Frederick William Janssen

History of American amateur athletics

Frederick William Janssen

History of American amateur athletics

ISBN/EAN: 9783337204235

Printed in Europe, USA, Canada, Australia, Japan

Cover: Foto ©Andreas Hilbeck / pixelio.de

More available books at **www.hansebooks.com**

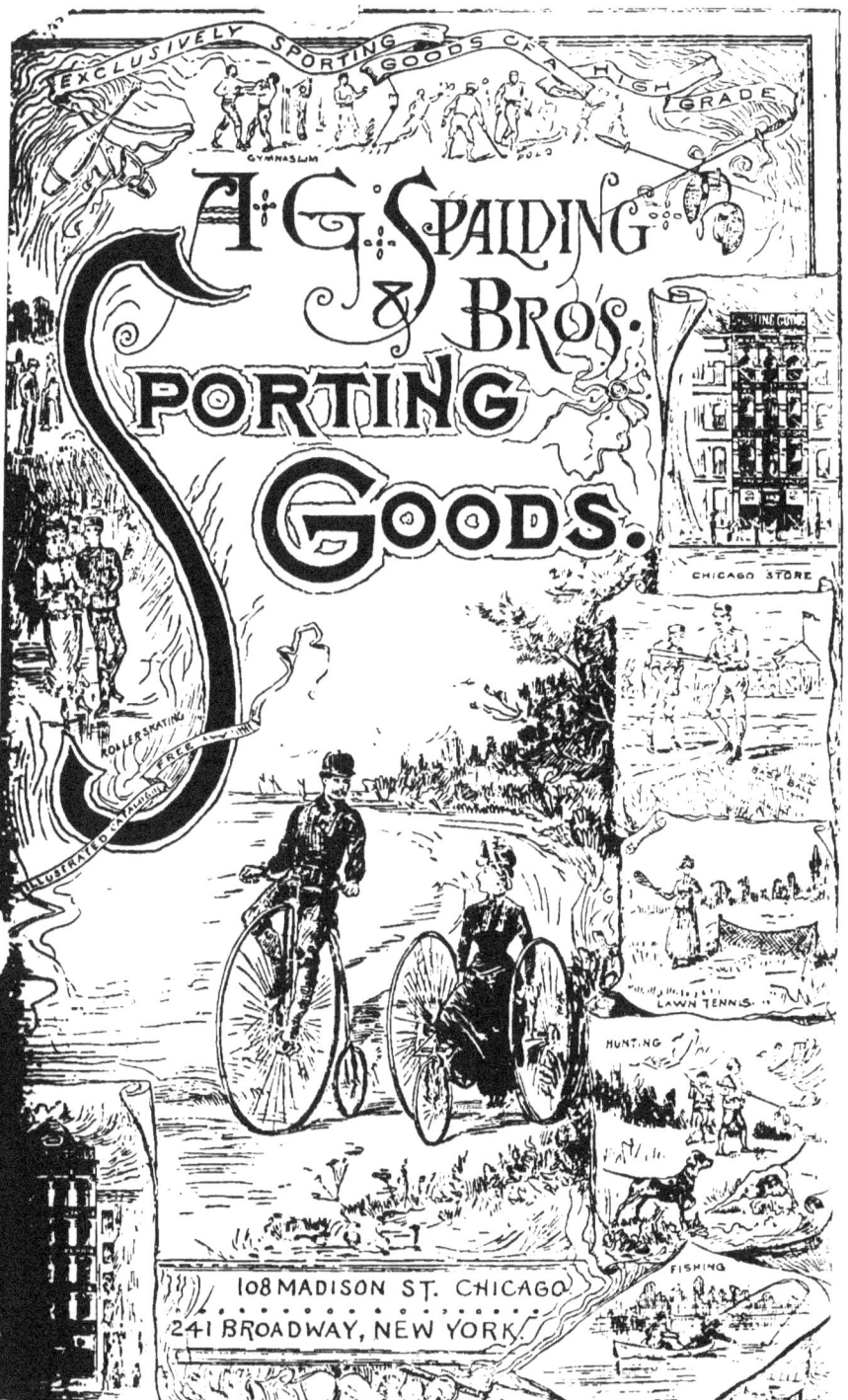

McCUE BROS.,
HATTERS

No. 178 Broadway,

Between Maiden Lane and John Street,

NEW YORK.

FIRST-CLASS GOODS ONLY.

We manufacture the Uniform Caps for all the Yachting and Boating Clubs around New York.

IF YOU WANT A

STYLISH AND FINE HAT

GIVE US A CALL.

SEND FOR THE
ILLUSTRATED CATALOGUE
OF
FIRE WORKS
—OF—

The Unexcelled Fireworks Co.,
No. 9 & 11 PARK PLACE, N. Y.

Western Depot, 519 Locust St., St. Louis, Mo.

LARGEST MANUFACTURERS.

Only Importers and Leading House in the Trade.

A SPECIALTY—Flags and Decoration Goods.

HOWE SCALE CO.,
RUTLAND,
VERMONT.

SCALES OF EVERY VARIETY,

PAGE, DENNIS & CO.,

AGENTS,

325 BROADWAY, NEW YORK.

HISTORY
—of—
American Amateur Athletics

COMPILED BY
FREDERICK W. JANSSEN
1885

PUBLISHED BY
CHARLES R BOURNÉ,
Printer and Stationer,
100 William Street,
New York.

-THE-
MANHATTAN LIFE INSURANCE CO.
OF NEW YORK,
156 & 158 BROADWAY,

Has Accumulated Assets of over $11,000,000, with Surplus of $2,300,000 by New York Standard.

"I MUST DIE TO WIN."

This is a common expression, used frequently in connection with Life Insurance as an objection to the ordinary life plan. "It is an excellent form of provision for the family, but I must die to win." But

YOU MAY LIVE AND WIN.

This refers to the Endowment plan, which meets the above objection. Take for instance, a policy payable to yourself 10, 15, or 20 years hence. If you die before the termination of the period, YOUR FAMILY WINS. If you survive the period, the policy becomes at once a provision for your own advancing years. YOU HAVE LIVED AND WON.

The "Manhattan's" new plan meets the want. It retains the advantage of the Endowment feature while reducing the net cash of Life Insurance under the contract to almost nothing.

For an example of the operation of this plan, address the Company, giving your age, and a statement will be sent you.

ORGANIZED IN 1850.

HENRY STOKES, President.

JACOB L. HALSEY, First Vice-President,   H. Y. YEMPLE, Secretary,
HENRY B. STOKES, Second Vice-President,   S. N. STEBBINS, Actuary.

THOMAS J. CONROY,
65 FULTON ST., NEW YORK.

Trade Mark.

Established 1830.

Manufacturer, Importer, Wholesale and Retail Dealer in

FINE FISHING TACKLE AND CAMPING GOODS.

Send 25 cents for my 130 page Illustrated Catalogue and Hand Book for Sportsmen. Containing Hints and Directions for Fishing and Camping. Customers may deduct amount paid for Catalogue from first purchase if it amounts to $1.00 or more.

Stack
Annex
GV
583
J26h

CONTENTS.

Preface.	3
National Association of Amateur Athletes of America.	5
Definition of an Amateur Athlete and Notes on Championship Games.	19
Best Amateur Records in America to October, 1885.	21
Best Amateur Records in England to October, 1885.	23
Amateur Champion Athletes of America—1876 to 1885.	24-28
New York Athletic Club.	31
Staten Island Athletic Club.	43
Williamsburgh Athletic Club.	63
Manhattan Athletic Club.	75
Hints on Exercising.	85
Table Showing the Digestibility of Food.	87
Definition of an Amateur Oarsman and Notes on Championship Regatta.	88
Amateur Champion Oarsmen of America—1873 to 1885.	89-91
Kill Von Kull Rowing Association.	92
Argonauta Rowing Association.	93
Viking Rowing Association.	94
Bayonne Rowing Association.	95
Newark Bay Boat Club.	97
Staten Island Rowing Club.	99
Clifton Boat Club.	100
Bayonne Canoe Club.	101
Hints on Canoeing.	102
Athletic Notes and Facts—1885.	103

FOR ANY KIND OF
MEDAL
—OR—
BADGE
APPLY TO

Jens F. Pedersen,
WATCHES,
Diamonds and Jewelry,
13 Maiden Lane,
NEW YORK.

Send 2-cent stamp for Illustrated Catalogue and Price-List.

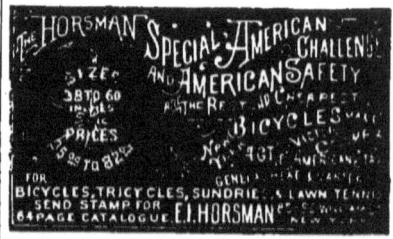

NICHOLAS C. MILLER,
President.

JOHN R. SMITH,
Vice-President.

JAS. M. HODGES,
Secretary.

THE WASHINGTON LIFE INSURANCE COMPANY.

W. A. BREWER, Jr., President.
W. HAXTUN, Vice-Pres. and Sec'y. CYRUS MUNN, Ass't Sec'y. E. S. FRENCH, Supt. of Agencies.
I. C. PIERSON, Actuary. B. W. McCREADY, M. D., Medical Ex'm'nr. FOSTER & THOMSON, Attys.

The Washington Life Insurance Company aims to protect the interest of its policy-holders from the date of their entrance to the maturity of their policies, and no other company uses better means to do this, or has succeeded so well. A reference here to a few of the salient features of their system will not be amiss.

A record under oath of the premium notices required by law is kept that can be referred to at any time, and in addition to this, and the usual notices sent by the company, a third notice is sent to all delinquents when premiums are due and unpaid. This makes the notification complete, and prevents any possible oversight on the part of the policy-holders.

Paid-up insurance upon the surrender of the policy is provided for by statute and is applicable to all companies alike, although the "Washington" gives more than required by law in cases of surrender of limited payment policies.

A cash value after three years is given at any time upon a proper release of the company's obligation, no limit being imposed as to specified periods of time, more or less remote.

Loans are made by the "Washington" on policies which have acquired a value of over $100, at the legal rate of interest, and upon the execution of the proper form of note furnished for such cases, provided the policy is not in favor of the wife, and is not a paid-up policy. The advantage of this is patent to all.

Dividends are declared annually at the end of the first year and each succeeding year, and may be drawn in cash at any time if premium on the policy is paid to date of draft.

Dividends not drawn are voluntarily and invariably applied by the company to keep the insurance in force if the premiums are unpaid, and during the time the policy is so held the insured may pay the balance of premium in cash without a medical re-examination.

Among all the insurance companies no other offers such a combination of advantages to the assured as this.

In a matter of such vital importance to all as life insurance, and where so many schemes—some good and many bad—present themselves, it is proper to use the utmost care and judgment in deciding where and how to insure. Insurance is and should be a legitimate business, based upon the experience and observation of years, and it is wisest to insure in such a company as does business on the soundest principles and has a good record for a guarantee.

Office 21 COURTLANDT STREET, NEW YORK.

PREFACE.

In presenting this book, it must be stated that, to give a complete history of American Amateur Athletics would be almost an impossibility, owing to the many branches of sports and innumerable organizations throughout the country.

This, however, has not been attempted, and the reader must bear in mind that this edition is a history in itself only so far as it goes, while the accounts of Clubs, Associations, Champions and Records belong merely to a few classes of sports such as Running, Walking, Rowing, Jumping, Bicycle Riding and Handling Weights.

The majority of the Club Histories contained herein have been prepared especially for this book, and the assistance of personal friends throughout the many different organizations is hereby gratefully acknowledged.

New York, November 1st, 1885.

(See *Notice* on last page.)

Inquire for

BOUCHÉ
Champagne "SEC"

To be had of the leading Wine Merchants and Grocers throughout the United States.

THE ONLY

GENUINE VICHY

Is from the SPRINGS owned by the FRENCH GOVERNMENT.

HAUTERIVE
   AND
CELESTINS, } Prescribed for the Gout, Rheumatism Diabetes, Gravel. Diseases of the Kidneys, etc., etc.

GRANDE GRILLE,—Diseases of the Liver.

HOPITAL,—Diseases of the Stomach, Dyspepsia.

To be had of all respectable Wine Merchants, Grocers and Druggists.

THE

NATIONAL ASSOCIATION

—OF—

AMATEUR ATHLETES OF AMERICA.

EARLY in 1879 the New York Athletic Club decided to give up the management of the Amateur Championship meeting so successfully established by them three years before. These games had been profitable, but brought a great deal of work on the officers of the club, who were continually being appealed to for decisions on athletic law, for information as to when the championship games would be given, and as to the programme, number of entries, ability of contestants, etc., etc., *ad infinitum*. This actually forced the club, in advertising its games, to request would-be contestants not to call on officers of the Club at their places of business. For these reasons, the Club was willing to deliver the conduct of the championship games to a properly organized association of athletic clubs. While the Club was still undecided as to the best form of a call for a meeting of such clubs to discuss the formation of an association, the matter was taken in hand by several gentlemen who had been prominent in athletic circles, but who had not been identified with the management of the strongest athletic clubs. Prominent among these were Messrs. Goodwin and White. Mr. Goodwin had been stroke of the four-oared crew of Columbia College, New York, who had been victorious at Henley, England, and had successfully conducted games in Madison Square Garden, New York, for the benefit of his college boat club. Mr. White was one of the best amateur walkers of his day, but had not done much athletic work for several years. These gentlemen favored an association formed of clubs whose standing, financial and social, was of the highest character, but several of which were not, actually speaking, athletic clubs. After a preliminary conference, a meeting was held at the Gilsey House, New York City, at which Messrs. Goodwin, White and several others met representatives of the prominent athletic clubs. These latter contended that in forming an association the clubs owning or leasing running

COMMUNICATE WITH

→❋ HEADQUARTERS ❋←
For Men's Furnishings and
ATHLETIC ⁘ EQUIPMENTS.

LARGEST ASSORTMENT.   POPULAR PRICES.

Gents' Dress Shirts,
" Neckwear,
Gents' Underwear,   Gents' Hosiery,
" Gloves,   " Jewelry.

—❋ SPECIAL ATHLETIC DEPARTMENT. ❋—

Estimates and designs furnished for CLUB | Orders by Mail carefully filled by parties
UNIFORMS and manufactured at Stock Prices. | understanding all the requirements in this line.

SOLE IMPORTERS OF THE FAMOUS
"DANIELL'S OLYMPIC" ATHLETIC SHIRT.
Daniell & Sons,
Broadway, Eighth and Ninth Sts., N. Y.

THE AMERICAN STAR BICYCLE.
A Practical Roadster, Safe from Headers or Other Dangerous Falls.

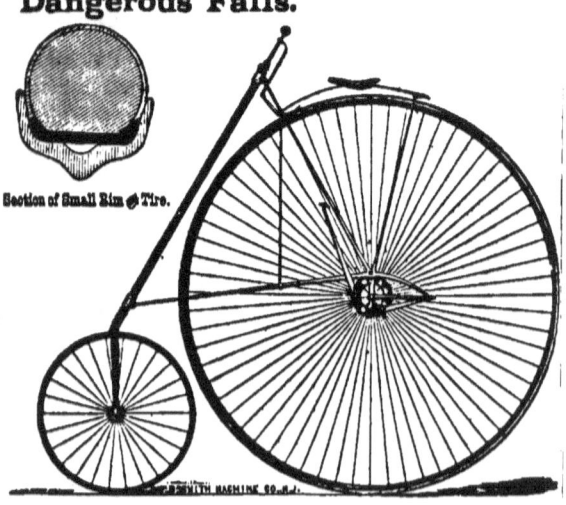

The means of propulsion insure a *continuous motion without dead centres*, a requisite condition for both speed and power.

The new *flat-seated* tires are a great improvement, and the new square grooved rim forms a wheel that will *not buckle.*

A "Reformed Crank Rider" says:—"In strength, safety, control, driving leverage, ease of motion, and coasting, the Star leads all Bicycles; while its positive action, quickness in steering and economy in pedaling are excluded from any other similar vehicle."

The workmanship and entire practicability of each and every machine are fully guaranteed.

For further particulars address,

H. B. SMITH MACHINE CO.,
SMITHVILLE,
Burlington County, N.J.

paths, or enclosed grounds, should form such association, and that boat, lacrosse and cricket clubs should not be entitled to a voice in such organization. A motion to this effect having been carried, by a very close vote, an association was formed under the name of the "National Association of Amateur Athletes of America," with George W. Carr, of the Manhattan Athletic Club, as President; O. T. Johnson, of the Staten Island Athletic Club, as Vice President; C. H. Truax, of the New York Athletic Club (now Judge of the Supreme Court of the State of New York), as Secretary, and Otis G. Webb, of the Plainfield Athletic Club, as Treasurer. Soon after permanent organization had been effected, the qualification for membership was changed, so that any athletic club giving a meeting with not less than five events open to all amateurs became eligible for admission. It was decided that any club failing to give at least once a year such a meeting should forfeit its membership in the Association.

The first championship meeting under the management of the Association was held on the 27th of September, 1879, on the New York Athletic Club grounds, Mott Haven, New York City, and was a decided success, the events being well contested and the audience large and enthusiastic.

The programme was as follows :

Running 100 Yards.
Running 220 Yards.
Running One-Quarter Mile.
Running One-Half Mile.
Running One Mile.
Running Three Miles.

Hurdle Racing, 120 yards, 10 hurdles, 3 feet 6 inches.
Walking One Mile.
Walking Three Miles.
Walking Seven Miles.
Running High Jump.
Running Broad Jump.
Pole Leaping.
Putting the Shot, 16 lbs.
Throwing the Hammer, 16 lbs.
Throwing 56 lbs. Weight.
Bicycle Racing, Two Miles.
Individual Tug of War.
Tug of War, teams of Five Men.

☞ **Dry Goods Delivered Free.**

E. J. DENNING & CO.

SUCCESSORS TO

A. T. STEWART & CO.,
(RETAIL.)

——)(DEALERS IN)(——

FOREIGN AND DOMESTIC DRY GOODS

OF EVERY DESCRIPTION.

**Silks, Satins, Velvets,
Plushes, Dress Goods, Cloaks,
Suits, Wraps, Shawls, Hosiery,
Underwear, Linens, Housekeeping
Goods, Furs, Millinery, Ribbons,
Gloves, Lace Curtains, Upholstery,
Fancy Goods, Notions, etc., etc.**

All *Dry Goods* bought of us (which will be sold at the LOWEST PRICES in the city), will be forwarded to any accessible point in the United States *Free of all Mail or Express Charges.*

☞ Orders by mail, for goods or samples, shall have prompt and careful attention.

Broadway, 4th Ave., 9th and 10th Streets,

NEW YORK.

JOHN D. LENNON,

Manufacturing Jeweler,

142 FULTON STREET,

NEW YORK.

Masonic, College, School, Athletic, Firemen's and Fine Presentation Medals & Jewels of Every Description.

FINE PRESENTATION MEDALS AND JEWELS A SPECIALTY.

☞ Designs furnished upon application.

BEST ON RECORD IN AMERICA.

At Championship Games, to September 24, 1879.

GAMES AND RECORD.	NAMES.	OF WHAT CLUB.	YEAR
Running 100 yds..............10 sec....	W. C. Wilmer.......	Short Hills A. C.	'78
Running 100 yds..............10 sec....	R. L. Montague......	N. Y. A C........	'78
Running 220 yds.........23¾ sec....	L. E. Meyers.........	M. A. C............	'76
Running 440 yds.........49 1-5 sec...,	L. E. Meyers.........	M A. C..........	'79
Running half-mile ......2m 2 4-5s....	Edward Merritt......	N. Y. A. C.........	'77
Running one mile......4m 37 2-5s....	Wm. J. Duffy........	H. A. C............	'79
Running three miles....16m 21½s...	E C. Stimson.........	Dart'h Coll........	'76
Hurdle racing 120 yds.........17⅛s....	H. Edwards Ficken.	N. Y. A. C.......	'78
Walking one mile........6m 44½s....	T. H. Armstrong....	H. A. C............	'77
Walking three miles ......21m 42s....	T. H. Armstrong....	H. A. C............	'78
Walking seven miles ... 55m 36½s....	W. H. Purdy.........	Greenp't A. C....	'79
Running high jump.........5f 8¼in...	J. P. Conover.........	C. Coll. A. Ass...	'79
Running broad jump.....21f 2½in....	W. C. Wilmer........	S. H. A. C........	'79
Pole leaping.........10f 5⅝in....	W. Van Houten......	S Am. A. C.......	'79
Putting the shot.........37f 10in....	—— Cuzner...........	McG Univ.........	'78
Throwing the Hammer .. 87f 1in....	F. Larkin...............	Princeton C.A.A.	'79
Throwing 56 lb wt........23f 1¼in....	William B. Curtis...	N. Y. A. C........	'79
Bicycle race, 2m............6m 59½s....	S. B. Pomeroy.......	Manhattan A. C..	'79

The annual meeting of the Association was held in the evening, and the following officers were elected: President, George W. Carr, of the Manhattan Athletic Club; Vice President, M. M. Forrest, of the Scottish Am. Athletic Club; Secretary, A. H. Curtis, of the New York Athletic Club; Treasurer, Otis G. Webb, of the Plainfield Athletic Club; Executive Committee—E. A. Rollins, of the Staten Island Athletic Club; John Gath, of the American Athletic Club; W. J. Tate, of the Jersey City Athletic Club; Harry M. Howard, of the Union Athletic Club (Boston). A resolution was passed that no person be allowed to compete at championship meetings who had not been connected for three months with a club whose standing was approved by the Executive Committee of the Association.

In 1880 the championship games were held on the New York Athletic Club grounds, at Mott Haven, on September 25.

GENUINE UNMIXED OLIVE OIL.

(The Finest in America.)

CARLO-OTTAVIO CORTI, LUCCA.

Olio d'Oliva Extra Soprafino,

(*Huile Douce et Delicate*)

De Possel Fils, (Established since 1820,)

EXTRA SUPERFINE VIERGE.

APPLY TO

Messrs. JANSSEN & CO., Agents,

No. 68 BROAD STREET,

P O. Box 125.   NEW YORK CITY.

THE NATIONAL ASSOCIATION OF A. A. A. 11

The clubs forming the Association were as follows :

AMERICAN ATHLETIC CLUB,	New York City, N Y.
CLINTON ATHLETIC CLUB,	Brooklyn, N. Y.
ELIZABETH ATHLETIC CLUB,	Elizabeth, N. J.
EMPIRE CITY ATHLETIC CLUB,	New York City, N. Y.
HARLEM ATHLETIC CLUB,	New York City, N. Y.
JERSEY CITY ATHLETIC CLUB,	Jersey City, N. J.
MANHTTAN ATHLETIC CLUB,	New York City, N. Y.
NEW YORK ATHLETIC CLUB,	New York City, N. Y.
OLYMPIC ATHLETIC CLUB,	San Francisco, Cal.
PLAINFIELD ATHLETIC CLUB,	Plainfield, N. J.
SCOTTISH AMERICAN ATHLETIC CLUB,	New York City, N. Y.
SHORT HILLS ATHLETIC CLUB,	Short Hills, N. J.
STATEN ISLAND ATHLETIC CLUB,	West New Brighton, N. Y.
UNION ATHLETIC CLUB,	Boston, Mass.

BEST AMATEUR RECORDS IN AMERICA.

At Championship Games, to August 1, 1880.

GAME.	RECORD.	NAME.	CLUB.
100 Yards Run	10sec	W. C. Wilmer	Short Hills A. C. '78
	10sec	R. L. La Montagne	New York A. C...'78
220 Yards Run	22¾sec.	L. E. Meyers	Manhattan A. C...'79
440 Yards Run	49 1 5sec	L. E. Meyers	Manhattan A. C..'79
Half-Mile Run	1min 56½sec.	L. E. Meyers	Manhattan A. C..'80
One Mile Run	4min 29½sec.	L. E. Meyers	Manhattan A. C .'80
Five-Mile Run	27min 55¾sec	W. H. Robertson	Brooklyn A. C....'80
120 Yds. Hurdle Race	17¼sec	H. Edwards Ficken	New York A. C..'78
One-Mile Walk	6m 33 2-5sec.	E. E. Merrill	Union A C........'80
Three-Mile Walk	21min 42sec.	T. H. Armstrong, jr.	Harlem A. C......'78
Seven-Mile Walk	55min 36½sec	W. H. Purdy	Greenpoint A. C.'79
Running High Jump	5feet 8¼ins.	J. P. Conover	Col. Coll. A. C....'79
Running Broad Jump	21feet 8ins.	J. S. Voorhees	Brooklyn A. C....'90
Pole Leaping	10feet 7¾ins.	B. F. Richardson	Scot. Am. A. C....'80
Putting the Shot	38feet 2¼ins.	J. A. Fullerton	Montreal L. C.....'80
Throwing the Hammer	87feet 1inch.	F. Larkin	Princeton C. A. A.'79
Throwing 56lb. Weight	23feet 1¼ins.	William B. Curtis	New York A. C...'79
Bicycle Race, 2 miles	6min 27sec	W. S. Clark	N. Y. Bicycle C..'80

Mercantile and Artistic Stationery.

Crane's Fine Writing Paper,

Distaffs' Super. Grecian Antique, Parchment Vellum,

All Linen, Overland,

Quadrille, Buckram, etc.,

OTHER FANCY PAPERS IN WHITE, CREAM OR AZURE.

IMPERIAL PURE IRISH and BELFAST LINEN PAPER.

MARCUS WARD & CO'S ROYAL IRISH LINEN.

Wedding Cards and Invitations a Specialty.
Only the VERY BEST STOCK and LATEST STYLES used, REASONABLE PRICES.

MONOGRAMS, CRESTS, COAT OF ARMS, ETC.,
☞ EXECUTED IN A FIRST-CLASS MANNER. ☜

VISITING CARDS ENGRAVED AND PUT IN A NEAT CASE,
Only $1.25 for 50 Cards and Plate.

BIRTHDAY CARDS ALWAYS IN STOCK,
Christmas, New Year, Valentine, and Easter Cards in Season.

Fine Printing and Lithographing of every description, Checks, Notes, Drafts, Receipts, Letter, Note, and Bill Heads, Memorandums, Circulars Pamphlets, Cards, Envelopes, etc.

ALL KINDS OF BLANK BOOKS ON HAND AND MADE TO ORDER.

CHARLES R. BOURNE,
STATIONER, PRINTER and BLANK BOOK MANUFACTURER,
100 WILLIAM STREET, N. Y.

THE NATIONAL ASSOCIATION OF A. A. A.

At the annual meeting, the officers elected were A. H. Curtis, President, of the New York Athletic Club ; E. A. Rollins, Vice President, of the Staten Island Athletic Club ; M. M. Forrest, Secretary, of the Scottish American Athletic Club ; Otis G Webb, Treasurer, of the Plainfield Athletic Club.

On September 25, 1881, the championship meeting was again held at Mott Haven. The following clubs had become members during the year : Baltimore, Montclair, Orion (Jersey City), Passaic (N. J), Rye (N. Y.), Williamsburg (Brooklyn, N. Y.), and Young America Cricket Club (Philadelphia, Pa.)

The same officers were elected for 1881–'82. William McEwen, of the Manhattan Athletic Club, was elected official handicapper.

This year the programme was as follows :

1.—100 Yards Run, trials.
2.—Seven Mile Walk.
3.—Running High Jump.
4.—Throwing the Hammer.
5—Running Broad Jump.
6.—Putting the Shot.
7.—Pole Leaping.
8.—Throwing 56lb. Weight.
9.—100 Yards Run, final.
10.—Bicycle Race, two miles.
11.—Half-Mile Run.
12.—Team Tug of War, trials. 5 men, 2 subs.
13.—One Mile Walk.
14.—440 Yards Run, trial.
15.—Five Mile Run.
16.—440 Yards Run, final.
17.—120 Yds Hurdle Race.
18.—Team Tug of War, final.
19.—120 Yards Hurdle Race, final
20.—220 Yards Run, trials.
21.—Individual Tug of War, trials.
22.—Three Mile Walk.
23.—220 Yards Run, final.
24.—Individual Tug of War, final.
25.—One Mile Run.

A. W. FABER,

LEAD PENCILS, GOLD PENS,

PENHOLDERS,

RUBBER BANDS AND RINGS,

THUMB TACKS,
TRACING CLOTH.

EBERHARD FABER,

718 & 720 BROADWAY,

NEW YORK.

21 Fulton Pier, West Washington Market;
47 WHITEHALL STREET;
New York City.

———DEALERS IN———

FRESH & SALTED MEATS.

POULTRY, GAME, ETC.,
IN SEASON.

BEST AMATEUR RECORDS IN AMERICA.

At Championship Games; to July 1, 1881.

GAME.	RECORD.	NAME.	CLUB.
100 Yards Run...............	10sec............	W. C. Wilmer........	Short H.A.C.'78
	10sec............	R. L. La Montagne.	N. Y. A.C...'78
	10sec............	L. E. Meyers........	M. A. C. ......'80
220 Yards Run......	22¼sec........	L. E. Meyers........	M. A. C. ......'79
440 Yards Run	40 1-5sec........	L. E. Meyers........	M. A. C. ......'79
Half Mile Run......	1min 56½sec.....	L. E. Meyers........	M. A. C. 80
One Mile Run	4min 29½sec	L. E. Meyers........	M. A. C. ......'80
Five Mile Run.	26min 44sec.....	J. H. Gifford........	Irish A. A. C. 81
120 Yds Hurdle Race....	17¼sec........	H. Ed. Ficken......	N. Y. A C....'78
One Mile Walk............	6min 33 2 5sec.	E. E. Merrill.........	Union A. C.... 80
Three Mile Walk	21min 42sec.....	T.H. Armstrong,jr.	Harlem A. C.'78
Seven Mile Walk....... ...	54min 7sec........	E. E. Merrill........	Scot. Am.A.C.'80
Running High Jump....	5ft 8¼in............	J. P. Conover.......	Col. Coll.A.A. 79
Running Broad Jump...	22ft 7¾in..........	J. S. Voorhees	M. A. C........'81
Pole Leaping................	10ft 11in..........	W. J. Van Houten.	Scot. Am.A.C.'80
Putting the Shot..........	38ft 2½in..........	J. A. Fullerton......	Montreal L. C. 80
Throwing the Hammer.	88ft 8 3-5in......	C.A.J.Queckberner.	Scot. Am.A.C.'80
Throwing 56lb. Weight.	24ft 4in.........	Jas. S. McDermott.	Scot. Am.A.C. 80
Bicycle Race, 2 miles ...	6min 27sec.......	W. S Clark..........	N.Y. B'cle C. 80

On March 4, 1882, it was decided to give the annual championship games on June 10, 1882, at the Polo Grounds, New York City, for the purpose of giving college athletes a better chance to contest. The games were given on that date, and at the annual meeting A. H. Curtis was re elected President; H. W. J. Telfair, Staten Island A. C., V.-President; G. H. Badeau, Williamsburgh A. C., Sec.; P. H. Charbock, Elizabeth A. C., Treas. The associate clubs were the Adelphi, American, Baltimore, Elizabeth, Manhattan, Montreal, New York, Olympic, Scottish-American, Staten Island, Union, Williamsburg and Inter-Collegiate Association. The events given this year were the same as in 1881, except team tug-of-war.

In 1883 the championship games were given June 2d, at Mott Haven, and the associate clubs were the same as in the year previous. G. H. Badeau was elected President; H. W. J. Telfair, V. Pres.; W. S. Sloan (Inter-Collegiate Association), Sec., and J. C. Wetmore (Elizabeth A. C.) Treas. The programme was essentially the same as in previous years.

W. A. COLLINS,
THE STATEN ISLAND REAL ESTATE BROKER,
26 PINE STREET, NEW YORK,
—AND—
NEW BRIGHTON, S. I.

FOR SALE.

At New Brighton, West New Brighton, Port Richmond, Clifton & Grymes' Hill,
Elegant Mansions, Cottages and Building Sites.
Also, Valuable Water Fronts.

TO LET.

At New Brighton and all accessible places on North and South Shores
FURNISHED AND UNFURNISHED HOUSES
Of every description.

P. FISHER,
MERCHANT TAILOR,
10 Whitehall Street,

OPPOSITE PRODUCE EXCHANGE. NEW YORK.

—THE BEST—

IMPORTED and
  AMERICAN WOOLENS
MADE UP AT THE LOWEST PRICES.
☞ FIT GUARANTEED.

On September 27, 1884, the ninth annual championship meeting was held on the grounds of the Williamsburgh Athletic Club, DeKalb avenue, Brooklyn, N. Y., the number and character of contests being about the same as the year before. At the annual meeting, held at the Metropolitan Hotel, N. Y., the ensuing evening, G. H. Badeau was re-elected President; E. G. Van Tambacht (American A. C.), V.-Pres.; J. M. Wainwright (Inter-Collegiate Association), Sec., and W. C. Wilmer (New York A. C.) Treas. G. D. Baird was elected official handicapper.

On March 21, 1885, an amended definition of an amateur, which had been prepared by a special committee appointed some time before, was submitted and, after slight alteration, adopted.

On April 30, 1885, arrangements were made with the League of American Wheelmen by which the bicycle rules of both associations became identical.

The championship meeting was held this year on the Manhattan Athletic Club grounds, New York City, on June 13, a slightly shorter programme being given.

ASSOCIATE CLUBS, 1885:

AMERICAN ATHLETIC CLUB, - - New York City, N. Y.
BALTIMORE ATHLETIC CLUB, - - - Baltimore, Md.
INTER-COLLEGIATE ATHLETIC ASSOCIATION, - ⎯⎯
MANHATTAN ATHLETIC CLUB, - - New York City, N. Y.
MISSOURI ATHLETIC CLUB, - - - - St. Louis, Mo.
NEW YORK ATHLETIC CLUB, - - New York City, N. Y.
OLYMPIC ATHLETIC CLUB, - - - New York City, N. Y.
PATERSON ATHLETIC CLUB, - - - - Paterson, N. J.
STAR ATHLETIC CLUB, - - - Long Island City, N. Y.
STATEN ISLAND ATHLETIC CLUB, West New Brighton, N. Y.
UNION AMATEUR ATHLETIC CLUB, - - Boston, Mass.
WILLIAMSBURGH ATHLETIC CLUB, - - Brooklyn, N. Y.

At the annual meetin G. H. Badeau was re-elected President; A. H. Curtis (New York A. C.), V.-Pres.; C. H. Mapes (Inter-Collegiate A. C.), Sec., and W. C. Rowland (Staten Island A. C.), Treas. W. G. Hegeman was elected official handicapper.

THE STATEN ISLAND ATHLETIC CLUB

HAVING PURCHASED

NEW GROUNDS,

(420 by 450 feet,)

WILL NEXT SEASON, PROVIDE FOR, and TAKE PART IN

BASE BALL, FOOT BALL,

LACROSSE, LAWN TENNIS,

AND **LADIES' SPORTS,** AS WELL AS

ATHLETIC GAMES,

SAILING AND ROWING.

HORACE L. HOTCHKISS & CO.,

Commission Stock Brokers,

No. 36 BROAD STREET, NEW YORK.

HORACE L. HOTCHKISS,
HARVEY B. RICH, } MEMBERS N. Y. STOCK EXCHANGE.

BRANCH OFFICES:
FIFTH AVENUE HOTEL,
WINDSOR HOTEL, } CONNECTED BY PRIVATE TELEGRAPH LINES.
MORTON HOUSE.

BOSTON, MASS.—BRANCH OFFICE, No. 59 CONGRESS STREET, REPRESENTED BY GEORGE C. BROOKS.

STOCKS AND BONDS BOUGHT OR SOLD ON MARGIN OR FOR CASH.

HAAS BROTHERS,

13 Avenue B,

BET. HOUSTON AND SECOND STS., · · NEW YORK.

—)(OPEN UNTIL 10 P. M.)(—

Special Department for ATHLETIC and GYMNASIUM OUTFITTINGS.

We make for the following Clubs:
NEW YORK ATHLETIC CLUB,
   NEW YORK RACKET CLUB,
      COLUMBIA COLLEGE, PRINCETON COLLEGE,
   NONPAREIL ROWING CLUB, NASSAU, UNION AND METROPOLITAN B. C.

We respectfully invite all who are in want of anything in our line to give us a call.

☞ SEND FOR PRICE LIST.

AN AMATEUR,

AS DEFINED BY THE NATIONAL ASSOCIATION.

An amateur is any person who has never competed in an open competition, for money, or under a false name, or with a professional for a prize, or where gate-money is charged; or has never at any time taught, pursued or assisted at athletic exercises for money, or for any valuable consideration.

CHAMPIONSHIP PRIZES.

A gold championship medal will be given to the winner in each contest, a silver medal to each winner of a second place, and a bronze medal to each winner of a third place.

CHAMPIONSHIP CLUB PRIZE.

A handsome stand of colors will also be presented to the club making the largest number of points, as follows: A winner in each contest will be entitled to five points, the second man three points, and the third man one point.

BEST ON RECORD PRIZES.

A special prize will be awarded to the competitor who shall beat an English record at an American championship game which has not been previously beaten in this country.

An entrance fee (not returnable) of two dollars per man, for each and every game, must accompany all entries, and in case any entry is accepted, the person entering will receive a competitor's ticket.

The committee reserve the right to refuse or strike out any entry.

Colors must be described in this order: First, color of handkerchief or cap; second, color of drawers.

Where clubs have adopted a special insignia, it will be noted in the programme.

Any competitor not a member of some recognized athletic or rowing organization must be properly introduced by some well-known person, who can vouch for his being an amateur.

PROGRAMME FOR CHAMPIONSHIP GAMES.

100-yards run, putting 16-lb. shot,
220-yards run, throwing 16-lb. hammer,
440-yards run, running high jump,
880-yards run, running broad jump,
120-yards hurdle, throwing 56-lb. weight,
1-mile run, pole-vaulting,
5-mile run, 1-mile walk,
3-mile walk, 4-mile bicycle race.

COLUMBIA BICYCLES AND TRICYCLES

Branch The Pope Manufacturing Co.,
12 WARREN ST., NEW YORK.

Standard Columbia.

Expert Columbia.

Columbia Light Roadster.

Columbia Racer.

Every part Interchangeable.

All parts kept in Stock.

Purchaser taught to Ride.

Finest Material and Workmanship.

Columbia Two-Track Tricycle, $160.

COLUMBIA RACER! 1 Mile record, 2 min. 38 3-5 sec.

Children's Velocipedes,
        Bicycles, and Petite Tricycles
——(ALSO KEPT IN STOCK.)——

SEND FOR ILLUSTRATED CATALOGUE.

ELLIOTT MASON, Manager.

BEST AMATEUR RECORDS IN AMERICA

To October 5th, 1885.

Event	Name	Club	Year	Record
100 Yards Run	L. E. Myers	Manhattan A. C.	1880	10 sec.
150 Yards Run	{ E. J. Wendell	Harvard College A. C.	1881	
	{ W. C. Wilmer	New York A. C.	1878	
220 "	R. L. La Montagne	New York A. C.	1878	22 2-5 sec.
300 "	H. S. Brooks, Jr.	Yale U. A. C.		15 1-8 sec.*
440 "	W. Baker	Harvard College		31 3-8 sec.
880 "	L. E. Myers	Manhattan A. C.		48 3-4 sec.
1 Mile Run	L. E. Myers	Manhattan A. C.		1 min. 55 2-5 sec.
1 Mile Run	W. G. George	Moseley H. England		4 min. 21 2-5 sec.
5 Mile Run	G. G. Smith	Williamsburgh A. C.		25 min. 30 2-5 sec.
1 Mile Walk	F. P. Murray			6 min. 29 3-5 sec.
3 Mile Walk	F. P. Murray	" "		21 min. 9 1-5 sec.
120 Yards Hurdle	T. Tivey			16 4-5 sec.
4 Mile Bicycle	L. B. Hamilton	Yale College A. C.		11 min. 55 2-5 sec.
Putting the Shot	F. C. Lambrecht	Manhattan A. C.		43 ft.
Throwing the Hammer	F. C. Lambrecht	Manhattan A. C.		96 ft. 10 in.
Throwing the 56-lb. Weight	C. A. J. Quackberner	New York A. C.		26 ft. 3 1-4 in.
Running High Jump	W. B. Page	University of Pennsylvania A. C.		6 ft. 1-4 in.
Running Broad Jump	J. S. Voorhees	Williamsburgh A. C.		22 ft. 7 3-4 in.
Pole-Vaulting	H. H. Baxter	New York A. C.		11 ft. 1-2 in.
Standing High Jump	W. Soren	New York A. C.		5 ft. 1-4 in.
Standing Broad Jump	M. W. Ford	New York A. C.		10 ft. 9 3-4 in.
Running Hop, Step and Jump	M. W. Ford	New York A. C.		44 ft. 1 3-4 in.

MARVIN'S SAFE CANNOT BE TAKEN APART WITH A COMMON SCREW DRIVER.

BELL'S HOMEOPATHIC PHARMACY,

3 Vesey St., "Astor House," New York.

HOMEOPATHIC BOOKS and MEDICINES.
EVERYTHING IN HOMEOPATHY.
Quality the Best—Popular Prices.

BELL'S COCOA, "The Strength Giver."—Unequalled for purity and flavor. Instantly prepared, not requiring to be boiled. A boon to mothers and children. Has received the endorsement of the Medical profession. Price—Small, 35 cents; 1 lb., 60 cents. Sent by mail free of postage.

BELL'S $3.50 MEDICINE CASE (Polished Wood).—Containing 20 3-dram square bottles Medicine, principal Homeopathic Remedies and book with full directions. *Sent free of express on receipt of price.*

BELL'S GUIDE TO HOMEOPATHY AND HEALTH (Medical Work.)—Free to any one on application.

OUR BAKERS AT WORK.

Sandwiches, Pies, Eclaires, etc.—uniform price, 5c. each. All our own make.

"VIENNA BUFFET," 21 NEW ST. AND 62 BROADWAY.

T. ASPINWALL & SON,

Tiles of all Descriptions for Floors, Walls, Hearths, Fireplaces, etc.

Wood Mantels, Open Fireplaces, Grates, Andirons, Brass Work, etc.

Designs and Estimates for work finished complete in any part of the Country.

75 & 77 West 23d St, New York.

BEST AMATEUR RECORDS. 23

BEST AMATEUR RECORDS IN ENGLAND

To October 5th, 1885.

Event	Name	Club	Year	Record
100 Yards Run	J. P. Tennant	Beauford House, London	1868	
	W. M. Tennant	Beauford House, London	1868	
	J. G. Wilson	Lillie Bridge, London	1871	
	A. J. Baker	London A. C.	1870	
	M. R. Portal	Balliol, Oxford	1879	10 sec.
	E. L. Lucas	Jesus Univesity A. C.	1880	
	F. G. L. Lucas	Trinity College A. C.	1880	
150 Yards Run	W. P. Phillips	London A. C.		15 sec.
220 "	W. P. Phillips	London A. C.		22 2-5 sec.
300 "	J. M. Cowie	London A. C.		31 4-5 sec.
440 "	L. E. Myers	Manhattan A. C.		48 3-5 sec.
880 "	L. E. Myers	Manhattan A. C.		1 min. 55 2-5 sec.
1 Mile Run	W. G. George	Moseley H.		4 min. 18 2-5 sec.
5 Mile Run	W. G. George	Moseley Harriers.		25 min. 7 4-5 sec.
1 Mile Walk	H. Whyatt	Notts Forest A. C.		6 min. 32 1-5 sec.
3 Mile Walk	H. Webster	Knotty Ash.		21 min. 28 sec.
120 Yards Hurdle	C. N. Jackson	O. U. A. C, and S. Palmer, C. U. A. C.		16 sec.
4 Mile Bicycle	G. L. Hillier	S. L. H.		11 min. 24 sec.
Putting the Shot	J. O'Brien	Dublin		44 ft. 10 1-2 in. (Irish record)
Throwing the Hammer	W. J. N. Barry	Queen's College, Cork		116 ft. 10 in. (Irish record)
Throwing the 56-lb. Weight	W. J. N. Barry	Queen's College, Cork		27 ft. (Irish record)
Running High Jump	P. Davin	Carrick-on-Suir		6 ft. 2 3-4 in. (Irish record)
Running Broad Jump	P. Davin	Carrick-on-Suir		23 ft. 2 in. (Irish record)
Pole-Vaulting	T. Ray	U. A. C.		11 ft. 4 1-2 in.
Standing High Jump				4 ft. 9 in.
Standing Broad Jump				10 ft. 5 in.
Running Hop, Step and Jump	J. Purcell			47 ft. 8 in.

MARVIN'S "FORGED ANGLE FRAME" **SAFE.**

AMATEUR CHAMPIONS OF AMERICA.

1876.

100 Yards Run............Fred'k. C. Saportas.New York City...........10½ sec.
440 Yards Run............Edward Merritt.........New York A. C.........54¼ sec.
Half-Mile Run............Harold Lambe..........Toronto, Canada...2 min. 10 sec.
One Mile Run ....Harold Lambe..........Toronto, Canada.4 min. 51½ sec.
120 Yards Hurdle Race. George Hitchcock.....New York City............?19 sec.
Running High Jump....H. Edwards Ficken...New York A. C.......5 ft. 5 in.
Running Broad Jump...Isaiah Frazier......... Yonkers Lyceum...17 ft. 4 in.
Putting the Shot..........H. E. Buermeyer.......New York A. C......34 ft. 5 in.
Throwing the Hammer.Wm. B. Curtis.........New York A. C......76 ft. 4 in.
One Mile Walk............D. M. Stern.............. New York A. C...7 min. 31 sec.
Three Mile Walk..........D. M. Stern.............New York A. C..25 min. 12 sec.
Seven Mile Walk..........Charles Connor.........New York City..58 min. 32½ sec.

1877.

100 Yards Run.............Charles C. McIvor......Montreal, Canada.........10⅛ sec.
220 Yards Run.............Edward Merritt.........New York A. C.............24 sec.
440 Yards Run.............Edward Merritt ....New York A. C...........55¼ sec.
Half-Mile Run ....R. R. Colgate.............New York A. C...2 min. 5⅜ sec.
One Mile Run...............Richard Morgan.........Harlem A. C......4 min. 49¾ sec.
120 Yards Hurdle Race. H. Edwards Ficken...New York A. C ....18¼ sec.
Running High Jump....H. Edwards Ficken...New York A. C........5 ft. 2 in.
Running Broad Jump...W. T. Livingston......Harlem A. C... .....18 ft. 9½ in.
Pole Leaping ....George McNichol......Scottish A. A. C .... 9 ft. 7 in.
Putting the Shot...........H. E. Buermeyer......New York A. C......87 ft. 2 in.
Throwing the Hammer.George D. Parmly. ..Princeton College A. C......84 ft.
One Mile Walk............E. C. Holske.............Harlem A. C...7 min. 11 4-5 sec.
Three Mile Walk..........E. C. Holske..... .....Harlem A. C...23 min. 9 2-5 sec.
Seven Mile Walk. ....T. H. Armstrong, Jr.Harlem A.C.55 min. 59 2-5 sec.

Tug of War.................. { Wm. B. Curtis, Captain. H. E. Buermeyer......... Austin Flint, Jr............ A. T. Heyn................. } New York A. C...40 sec.

MARVIN'S SAFES Have "Recessed Door with Book Case Protector."

AMATEUR CHAMPIONS OF AMERICA.
1878.

100 Yards Run..............W. C. Wilmer.........Short Hills A. C.............10 sec.
220 Yards Run.............W. C. Wilmer..........Short Hills A. C.........22⅞ sec.
440 Yards Run.............Frank W. Brown......Glenwood A. C............54¾ sec.
Half-Mile Run.............Edward Merritt.........New York A. C...2 min. 5¼ sec.
One Mile Run............ Thomas H. Smith....Manhattan A. C.4 min. 51¼ sec.
Three Mile Run ....William J. Duffy......Harlem A. C......17 min. 25 sec.
120 Yards Hurdle Race.H. Edwards Ficken...New York A. C.............17⅜ sec.
Running High Jump....H. Edwards Ficken...New York A. C.........5 ft. 5 in.
Running Broad Jump...W. C. Wilmer..........Short Hills A. C. .....18 ft. 9 in.
Pole Leaping.......... .....Alfred Ing...............Scottish Amer. A. C...9 ft. 4 in.
Putting the Shot.........H. E. Beurmeyer......New York A. C......37 ft. 4 in.
Throwing the Hammer.William B. Curtis......New York A. C......80 ft. 2 in.
Throwing 56 lb. Weight.William B. Curtis......New York A. C.. ....21 ft.
Three Mile Walk.........T. H. Armstrong, Jr.Harlem A. C..,.23 min. 12½ sec.

Tug of War........... { Maxwell E. More, Capt.
E. Arnold......... ....
C A J Quackberner...
Andrew L Thompson... } Scottish A. A. C. { 1st pull 51 sec ; final pull, 1 m 53¼ sec

1879.

100 Yards Run.............B. R. Value.............Elizabeth A. C.............10⅜ sec.
220 Yards Run............L. E. Myers.:............Manhattan A. C............23⅜ sec.
440 Yards Run.............L. E. Myers.............Manhattan A. C.......52 2-5 sec.
Half-Mile Run.............L. E. Myers.............Manhattan A. C.2 min. 1 2-5 sec.
One Mile Run.............H. M. Pellatt............Toronto L. C..4 min. 43 2-5 sec.
Three Mile Run............P. J. McDonald........Irish A. A. C..15 min 38 3-5 sec.
120 Yards Hurdle Race.J E. Haigh..............Scottish Amer. A. C......19 sec.
Running High Jump..W. Wunder.............Olympic A. C., Phila...5 ft. 7 in.
Running Broad Jump...F. J. Kilpatrick........New York A. C......19 ft. 6¾ in.
Pole Leaping...............W. T. Van Houten....Scottish A. A. C....10 ft. 4¾ in.
Putting the Shot..........A, W. Adams.........Scottish A. A. C....36 ft. 3½ in.
Throwing the Hammer.J. McDermott ....Scottish A. A. C....86 ft. 11⅛ in.
Throwing 56 lb.Weight.J. McDermott..........Scottish A. A. C....22 ft. 11 in.
One Mile Walk............W. H. Purdy............Greenpoint A. C..6 min 48¾ sec.
Three Mile Walk.........W. H. Purdy............Greenpoint A. C.22 min. 58¾ sec.
Seven Mile Walk.........E. E. Merrill ....Union A. C., Boston.56 m. 4 sec.
Bicycle Race, 2 miles...L. H. Johnson...........Essex B. C......... 7 min. 22 sec.

Tug of War, (teams of five) { Wm B Curtis, Captain...
J. C. Gillies....................
J. H. Walden..................
H. E. Buermeyer............
J. E. McNichol................ } New York A. C.
10 min. time limit.

Tug of War, (Individual) 5 min. time limit.   A. L. Thomson
                                                        Scottish Amer. A. C.

MARVIN'S "FORGED ANGLE FRAME" SAFE.

AMATEUR CHAMPIONS OF AMERICA.

1880.

100 Yards Run............L. E. Myers.............Manhattan A. C.......10 2-5 sec.
220 Yards Run............L. E. Myers............Manhattan A. C.......23 3-5 sec.
440 Yards Run............L. E. Myers............Manhattan A. C............52 sec.
Half Mile Run........ ....L. E Myers............Manhattan A. C. 2 min. 4 3-5 sec.
One Mile Run,........ ......H. Fredericks............Manhattan A. C. 4 m. 39 3-5 sec.
Five Mile Run...............J. H. Gifford............Irish A. A. C.. 27 m. 51 3-5 sec.
120 Yards Hurdle Race. H. H. Moritz............Scottish A. A. C......19 1-5 sec.
Running High Jump....A. L. Carroll............Staten Island A. C...... 5 ft. 5 in·
Running Broad Jump...J. S. Voorhees...........Manhattan A. C....... 21 ft. 4 in.
Pole Leaping...............W. J. Van Houten....Scottish Amer. A. C. 10 ft. 11 in.
Putting the Shot..........A. W. Adams...........Scottish Amer. A.C. 36 ft. 4¼ in.
Throwing the Hammer. W. B. Curtis............New York A. C.....87 ft. 4¼ in.
Throwing 56 lb. Weight.J. S. McDermott.......Scottish Amer. A. C.24 ft. 4 in.
One Mile Walk............E. E. Merrill ....Scottish A. A. C....7 min. 4 sec.
Three Mile Walk..........E. E. Merrill ....Scottish A. A. C..22 m. 28 4-5 s.
Seven Mile Walk......... J. B. Clark...............Empire City A. C.54 m. 47 3-5 s.
Bicycle Race, 2 miles...L. H. Johnson...........Manhattan A. C...6 m. 56 4-5 s.

Tug of War (team of five) { W. B. Curtis, Captain / J. W. Carter............... / J. H. Walden............... / H. E. Buermeyer .... / J. H. Montgomery..... } New York A. C.

Tug of War (Individual)......C. A. J. Quackberner.....Scottish Amer. A C

1881.

100 Yards Run............L. E. Myers............Manhattan A. C.......... 10¼ sec.
220 Yards Run............L. E. Myers............ Manhattan A. C. ....23½ sec.
440 Yards Run............ L. E. Myers............Manhattan A. C.......49 2-5 sec.
Half Mile Run ....Walter Smith............Williamsburg A. C. 2 min. 4 sec.
One Mile Run.............H. Fredericks..........Manhattan A. C.. 4 m. 32 3-5 sec.
Five Mile Run.............W. C. Davies............Williamsb'g A. C. 27 m. 43 4-5 s.
120 Yards Hurdle Race..J. A. Tivey..............Williamsburg A. C.......17⅘ sec.
Running High Jump....C. W. Durand..........Staten Island A. C.....5 ft. 8 in·
Running Broad Jump...J. S. Voorhees.. ....Manhatttan A. C...21 ft. 4¾ in.
Pole Leaping...............W. J. Van Houten....Scottish A. A. C......10 ft. 6 in.
Putting the Shot..........F. L. Lambrecht.......Pastime A. C.........37 ft. 5½ in.
Throwing the Hammer. F. L. Lambrecht.......Pastime A. C......... 89 ft. 8 in.
Throwing 56 lb. Weight.J. Britten................Scottish A. A. C............. 24 ft.
One Mile Walk............E. E. Merrill.............Union A. C., Boston .. 7 m. 2¾ s.
Three Mile Walk.........E. E. Merrill.............Union A. C., Boston. 23 m. 55¾ s.
Seven Mile Walk........W. H. Purdy............Manhattan A. C...... 58 m. 43 s.
Bicycle Race, 2 Miles...C. H. Reed..............New York A. ....\ 7 m. 6 ¼ s.

Tug of War............. { C. A. Berwin................ / C. P. Gaffney................... / M. Gorman..................... / R. Payton..................... / J. O. Stephens................ } Harlem A. C.

Tug of War (Individual) C. A. J. Quackberner........S. A. A. C.

Marvin Safe Co. NEW YORK, PHILADELPHIA AND LONDON.

AMATEUR CHAMPIONS OF AMERICA.

1882.

100 Yards....................A. Waldron.............Manhattan A. C..no time taken.
220 Yards....................H. S. Brooks, Jr.......Yale University A. C. 22 3-5 sec.
440 Yards....................L. E. Myers.............Manhattan A. C. ......51 3-5 sec.
880 Yards.................. W. H. Goodwin, Jr...New York A. C...1 m. 56¼ sec.
One Mile Run............H. Fredericks..........Manhattan A. C..4 m. 36 1-5 sec.
120 Yards Hurdle........J. A. Tivey...............Williamsb'g A. C......16 4-5 sec.
One Mile Walk............W. H. Parry............Williamsb'g A.C.7 m. 10 3-5 sec.
Three Mile Walk.........F. G. Trunkett........Williamsb'g A. C...24 m. 19 sec.
Seven Mile Walk.........F. P. Murray............Williamsb'g A. C..57 m. 18½ sec.
Putting the Shot..........F. L. Lambrecht......Pastime A. C.........39 ft. 9¼ in.
Throwing the Hammer,F. L. Lambrecht......Pastime A. C...........93 ft. ¼ in.
Running High Jump... A. L. Carroll............Staten Island A. C..... 5 ft. 7 in.
Running Long Jump....F. J Jenkins, Jr......New York A. C......21 ft. 5¾ in.
Pole Vaulting..............B. J. Richardson...... Scottish A. A. C........ .....10 ft.
Throwing 56 lb. Weight H. W. West. ....Boston Y. M. C. A..24 ft. 10¼ in.
Five Mile Run..............T. F. Delaney..........Gramercy A. C...37 m. 34 2-5 s.
Two Mile Bicycle.........G. D. Gideon...........Germantown B. C..6 m. 41 3-5s.
Five Mile Bicycle.........G. D. Gideon............Germantown B. C 17 m. 19 4-5 s.

Tug of War (team of five { C. A. Berwin.................. / C. P. Gaffney.......... . ... / M. Gorman .... / R. Payton...................... / O. J. Stephens................ } Harlem A. C.

Tug of War (Individual).......C. A. J. Quackberner......Scottish Amer. A. C.

1883.

100 Yards Run.............A. Waldron...........Manhattan A. C.........10¼ sec.
220 Yards Run............H. S. Brooks, Jr.......Yale U. A. C.........22 4-5 sec.
440 Yards Run........... L. E. Myers............Manhattan A. C........52⅛ sec.
880 Yards Run...........J. J. Murphy...........Manhattan A. C..2 m. 4 2-5 sec.
One Mile Run. ....H. Fredericks ....Manhattan A. C. 4 m. 36 4-5 sec.
120 Yards Hurdle.........S. A. Safford............American A. C........19 2-5 sec.
One Mile Walk............F. P. Murray............Williamsb'g A. C...6 m. 46 sec.
Three Mile Walk.........G. S. Baird...............American A. C.. 22 m. 8 3-5 sec.
Seven Mile Walk.........W. H. Meek.............West Side A.C. 56 m. 48 2-5 sec.
Putting the Shot..........F. L. Lambrecht.......Pastime A. C....................43 in.
Throwing the Hammer.W. L. Condon..........Baltimore A. C.......93 ft. 11 ft.
Running Long Jump....M. W. Ford.............New York A. C......21 ft. 7¼ in.
Running High Jump....M. W. Ford.............New York A. C.....5 ft. 8½ in.
Pole Vaulting..............H. H. Baxter............New York A. C.....11 ft. ⅜ in.
Throwing 56 lb. Weight.F. L. Lambrecht......Pastime A. C.........25 ft. 1¾ in.
Five Mile Run..............T. F. Delaney.........Williamsb'g A. C.26 m. 47 2-5 s.
Two Mile Bicycle ....G. M. Hendee..........S. B. C. ....6 min. 47 1-5 sec.
Five Mile Bicycle.........R. G. Rood.............Ixion B. C...17 min. 37 2-5 sec.
Tug of War (Individual) .... C. A. J. Quackberner......N. Y. A. C.

MARVIN'S FIRE & BURGLAR SAFES.

AMATEUR CHAMPIONS OF AMERICA.

1884.

Event	Athlete	Club	Performance
100 Yards Run	M. W. Ford	New York A. C.	10 4-5 sec.
220 Yards Run	L. E. Myers	Manhattan A. C.	24 1-5 sec.
440 Yards Run	L. E. Myers	Manhattan A. C.	55 4-5 sec.
880 Yards Run	L. E. Myers	Manhattan A. C.	2 min. 9 4-5 sec.
One Mile Run	P. C. Madeira	P. F. & S. A.	4 min. 36 4.5 sec.
120 Yards Hurdle	S. A. Safford	American A. C.	18 1-5 sec.
One Mile Walk	F. P. Murray	Williamsb'g A. C.	6 m. 54 3-5 s.
Three Mile Walk	F. P. Murray	Williamsb'g A. C.	23 m. 15 2-5 s.
Seven Mile Walk	E. F. McDonald	West Side A. C.	56 m. 28 s.
Putting the Shot	F. L. Lambrecht	Manhattan A. C.	39 ft. 10 in.
Throwing the Hammer	F. L. Lambrecht	Manhattan A. C.	92 ft. 5 in.
Running Long Jump	M. W. Ford	New York A. C.	20 ft. 1½ in.
Running High Jump	J. T. Rhinehardt	American A. C.	5 ft. 8 in.
Pole Vaulting	H. H. Baxter	New York A. C.	10 ft.
Throwing 56 lb. Weight	C. A. J. Quackberner	New York A. C.	26 ft. 3¼ in.
Five Mile Run	George Stonebridge	West Side A. C.	27 m. 45 sec.
Two Mile Bicycle	L. Hamilton	Waterbury, Conn.	6 m. 58 sec.
Five Mile Bicycle	L. Hamilton	Waterbury, Conn.	18 m. 36 sec.

1885.

Event	Athlete	Club	Performance
100 Yards Run	M. W. Ford	New York A. C.	10 3-5 sec.
220 Yards Run	M. W. Ford	New York A. C.	24 4-5 sec.
440 Yards Run	H. M. Raborg	New York A. C.	54 1-5 sec.
880 Yards Run	H. L. Mitchell	Yale College A. C.	2 m. 2 3-5 s.
One Mile Run	G. Y. Gilbert	Manhattan A. C.	4 m. 45 1 5 sec.
120 Yards Hurdle	A. A. Jordan	Manhattan A. C	17 3-5 sec.
One Mile Walk	G. D. Baird	Olympic A C	6 min. 42 sec.
Three Mile Walk	E. D. Lange	Manhattan A. C.	23 m. 10 3 5 s.
Seven Mile Walk	F. P. Murray	Williamsb'g A. C.	54 m. 31 1-5 s.
Putting the Shot	F. L. Lambrecht	Manhattan A. C.	42 ft. 2⅜ in.
Throwing the Hammer	F. L. Lambrecht	Manhat'an A. C.	96 ft. 10 in.
Running Long Jump	M. W. Ford	New York A. C.	21 ft. 6 in.
Running High Jump	W. B. Page	P. F. & S. A.	5 ft. 9¾ in.
Pole Vaulting	H. H. Baxter	New York A. C.	11 ft. 3 in
Throwing 56 lb Weight	C. A. J. Quackberner	New York A. C.	26 ft. 3 in.
Five Mile Run	P. D. Skillman	Manhattan A. C.	27 m. 13 2-5 s
Four Mile Bicycle	A. B. Rich	Staten Island A.C.	14 m. 2 2-5s
Tug of War (five men)	J. Van Houten, Captain; M. Mullhern; B. Cannon; T. Moran; T. Owens	West Side A. C.	

MARVIN'S SAFE — CANNOT BE TAKEN APART WITH A COMMON SCREW DRIVER.

HISTORIES

—OF THE—

NEW YORK, STATEN ISLAND, WILLIAMSBURGH AND MANHATTAN ATHLETIC CLUBS.

COMPILED, ARRANGED AND WRITTEN BY

FREDERICK W. JANSSEN,

WITH THE ASSISTANCE OF

G. H. BADEAU,	President N. A. A. A. A. and Williamsburgh A. C.
G. W. CARR,	President Manhattan A. C.
O T. JOHNSON,	Ex-President Staten Island A. C.
W B. CURTIS,	Ex-President New York A C.
L. E. MYERS,	Manhattan A. C. (Champion Runner of the World.)
WALTON STORM,	Captain Manhattan A. C.
A. B. RICH,	2d Lieutenant Staten Island A. C.
J. B. LIDDLE,	Treasurer Williamsburgh A. C.

BARTENS & RICE,

20 JOHN ST. (Up stairs), NEW YORK.

Watches of all Grades.

Artistic Designers of

ORNAMENTS OF GOLD AND PRECIOUS STONES.

MAKERS OF

ATHLETIC MEDALS
——AND——
SOCIETY BADGES.

DESIGNS FURNISHED.   INSPECTION INVITED.

~~~~~~~~~~~~~~~~~~~~~~~~~~~~~~~~~~~~

F. J. KALDENBERG,

MANUFACTURER OF
**MEERSCHAUM AND BRIAR PIPES,
CIGAR AND CIGARETTE HOLDERS, ETC.**

Smokers' Articles of every Description.

IVORY GOODS, BILLIARD AND POOL BALLS, WALKING CANES IN GREAT VARIETY.

125 Fulton Street,
6 Astor House, Broadway,   **NEW YORK.**

HISTORY OF THE
NEW YORK ATHLETIC CLUB,

NEW YORK CITY.

THE New York Athletic Club was born June 17, 1866, in the back parlor of No. 200 Sixth avenue, New York city (now a part of R. H. Macy & Co.'s store, but then a private residence), and its parents were :—

JOHN C. BABCOCK,
HENRY E. BUERMEYER,
WILLIAM B. CURTIS.

Babcock and Curtis—brothers since boyhood in everything save birth—had been for twelve years enthusiastic athletes, although athletic clubs and athletic meetings were as yet unknown. Unable to find associates, or competitions, or prizes, they nevertheless faithfully practiced running, walking, leaping, feats of strength, swimming and skating, solely for their own health and amusement. There being so many days in which the weather made it necessary to substitute indoor for outdoor sport, they fitted up their back parlor with dumbbells, clubs, lifting-machines, boxing-gloves and all the other paraphernalia of a first-class gymnasium, and snugly ensconced in this cozy shrine of manly sport, they successfully bade defiance to frost and storm.

The most frequent and welcome visitor at No. 200 Sixth avenue was Henry E. Buermeyer, of Brooklyn, whose personal prowess and ardent love of all manly sport made him a most congenial guest.

In 1866 amateur athletic sport had just begun to assume prominence in England. The first English amateur athletic club, the Mincing Lane—a name soon changed to the London Athletic Club—was founded in June, 1863; the first Oxford-Cambridge games were held March 5, 1864, and the first amateur championship meeting March 23, 1866. June 17, 1866, was a rainy Sunday, and in the parlor at 200 Sixth avenue, Babcock, Buermeyer and Curtis, enjoying

MARVIN'S SAFES HAVE THE **"Sliding Back Plate."**

needed rest after a half hour with the heavy weights, discussed the rapid rise and spread of athletic sports in England, and decided to begin at once an earnest and persistent endeavor to interest American youth in those matters, and eventually to found an American amateur athletic club on the model of its English predecessors. No. 200 Sixth avenue was chosen as the headquarters and weekly rendezvous.

Those whose acquaintance with amateur athletics dates back but a few years can hardly appreciate the coolness with which these sports were at first received here, and the difficulty experienced by these three athletic crusaders in inducing recruits to rally around their banner. Babcock was a member of the Nassau Boat Club, while his associates had seats in the racing crew of the Atlantic Boat Club. Naturally, the first to follow their lead were members of these two rowing clubs, but after a while outsiders began to drop in one by one.

When mud, snow or storm prevented outdoor work, the weekly reunion was limited to a half-day's session at 200 Sixth avenue. The participants, though few, were of high athletic rank, competition was spirited, and the greatest lifting feat on record is credited to one of these meetings.

Not only did the members thus amuse themselves, but that snug back parlor soon secured a national reputation as a sort of muscular assay office, where candidates for athletic honors could have their abilities accurately tested and their athletic rank definitely established. Did some rural village boast an Herculean dumb-bell lifter, he was escorted to 200 Sixth avenue, introduced to those three hollow dumb-bells—loading from 60 pounds to 200 pounds—and went home knowing the exact difference between his actual and his reputed strength. Did newspapers report some Samsonian club-swinger, he was straightway confronted with those jointed clubs—loading from 12 pounds to 100 pounds—and speedily enabled to prove the limit of his powers. Was there somewhere a famous lifter, he was decoyed sooner or later into the trap, mounted on the old ash lifting-table, and allowed to learn for himself the remarkable difference between lifting weighed pounds and guessed pounds. Did the friends of some stalwart boxer become a trifle boisterous in his boasts, he was invited to the back parlor, and permitted to display his talent to his heart's content in mimic battle with that suave and gentle giant, H. E. Buermeyer. A strict regard for historic truth makes necessary the admission that there is no authentic record of any instance in which an aspirant for fistic honors returned for a second lesson. The carefulness and exactness with which these trials were conducted soon gained public recognition, and for several years the fact that any feat had been

MARVIN'S FIRE & BURGLAR **SAFES.**

accomplished at No. 200 Sixth avenue was a Hall-mark which stamped the performance as sterling silver.

Whenever the weather permitted, the parlor was abandoned and sport pursued in the open air. The first rendezvous was on the half-mile track connected with the old "Red House," Mark Maguire's famous roadside hostelry, at the head of Harlem lane. Here, after running the half-mile circuit in 2m. 30s., or walking it in 5m.—feats then considered worthy of note—the fathers of the club, thoroughly exhausted by such extraordinary efforts, would throw themselves on the grass for a half-hour's rest, and then spend another thirty minutes in conversation with that quaint Yorkshireman, James McKay, who had established a boat-building shop in the second story of Maguire's stable, and was just then hard at work on the first genuine racing-shell ever built in the United States.

In a few months the march of improvement ran a street and a row of tenements through the middle of the track, and a change was made to the Elysian Fields, Hoboken. There was no regular track, but a good quarter-mile circuit could be marked out on the level turf of the ball field, and several straightaway 100-yard courses on the shore path. Here the regular attendants were joined by many members of the Atlantic Boat Club, whose boat-house was only a quarter of a mile below. Many spirited contests took place, and in one ever-memorable handicap one of the founders of the club was credited with running 102 yards in 9 seconds—a signal triumph of watch-holding over truth.

To this comfortable and convenient trysting-place there were two objections: there was no regular track, and the Fields being then the people's pleasure-ground, much as Coney Island is now, the crowds of curious spectators were always annoying and sometimes aggressive. So a removal was made to Finley's half-mile track, corner of 72d street and the Bloomingdale road. These grounds proved to be eminently desirable. The proprietor—a jolly, sport-loving old Englishman—did everything in his power to make his visitors comfortable, and no further change was made till the summer of 1871, when the club opened its own grounds in Harlem. On Finley's pleasant grounds weekly games were held whenever weather permitted. The Atlantic Boat Club men rowed across from their Hoboken quarters, beached their barges at the foot of 73d street, climbed the steep bluff of what is now Riverside Park, and joined in the contests, while the Nassau Boat Club party paddled up from their boat-house, foot of 34th street and North River, and the New York city contingent came up by the Eighth avenue street-cars.

During the summer of 1868 forty-three persons were registered

---

MARVIN SAFE CO., ESTABLISHED 47 YEARS.

as having participated in three or more of these reunions, and the average weekly attendance was about twenty. These results, insignificant as they now appear, then gave great satisfaction, and were thought sufficient to warrant the permanent organization and incorporation of an amateur athletic club. A meeting was called, notices published in daily and sporting journals, and written invitations sent to all who had ever attended any of the weekly sports; but, despite this timely publicity, only seven persons assembled, and an adjournment was promptly made. A second trial, three weeks later, resulted similarly, and it was not until the third attempt (September 8, 1868,) that fourteen faithful ones could be gathered together to sign a muster roll, elect officers, appoint committees and complete the formal organization of America's first amateur athletic club. .

Being now a full-fledged athletic club, it was, of course, necessary to give a regular open amateur athletic meeting, and the management was entrusted to a games committee. Athletic games and cinder-paths were then unknown in America, and Finley's track, though pleasant enough for practice, was out of the way and inaccessible for spectators. Fortunately, Mr. Babcock was just then building for the Third Avenue Railroad Company the structure now known as the American Institute Rink, and it was decided to hold the games in that building Wednesday evening, November 11, 1868 Contractor and builder were dilatory, as usual; the morning of November 11 broke cold and stormy; the building was not yet half-roofed, and the committee, scouring West and South streets with wagons, accumulated a quarter-acre of tarpaulins and made a temporary roof, under which the games were successfully contested. The central section of the Rink had not been floored, and an eighth-of-a-mile path was staked out on the smooth clay surface.

In America amateur athletic circles there was at that time only one pair of spiked shoes, bought by W. B. Curtis in one of London's by-ways. They were clumsy, long-toed, and of such generous proportions as best fitted their owner's ample feet. No one then knew anything about those new-fangled weapons, but everybody agreed that if they were in common use by English athletes, they must be desirable for Americans. So everybody wished for a pair; everybody coveted this pair; everybody envied their fortunate possessor, and everybody wished to borrow them. Their complaisant owner tried to satisfy all, and succeeded in distributing these shoes quite widely. After he had worn them in the 75-yard and 220-yard runs, H. J. Magrane used them in the quarter-mile and half-mile runs, H. E. Buermeyer in the hammer-throwing and shot-putting, and finally, strangest of all, they carried J. E. Russell to victory in the one-mile walk.

MARVIN'S ARE THE BEST SAFES.

The contestants at the first American open amateur meeting included all the young men in the neighborhood of New York city who had ever developed ability in any branch of athletic sport. Not only did the programme show the names of all the active members of the new club and all their acquaintances who were able to exhibit good performance at running, walking, leaping, or feats of strength, but a special invitation, or rather challenge, was extended to the New York Caledonian Club, then, as now, the most prominent of American Caledonian societies, and their most eminent athletes were present to compete, thus making the affair an international match—America against Scotland. The result was, as might have been foreseen, America won the running and walking contests, while Scotland was successful with the hammer and shot, and in pole-leaping, standing high jump and running long jump—the games most common at Caledonian meetings.

The many thousand bicyclists of to-day will be interested in learning that at this meeting was given the first public exhibition of the newly-invented velocipede—now known as "The Boneshaker"—which was the forerunner of the modern bicycle. The leading sporting journal of that day reported the event as follows :

"At this juncture the velocipede race, which the programme announced as the closing feature of the exercises, took place. It proved nothing more—nor was it intended to be more—than an exhibition of the speed to be gained by these wonderful engines of locomotion. The carriage consists of but two wheels, placed one before the other, with a treadle apparatus to spin them on. Without speaking a word about the velocity with which one can cover ground while riding this machine, the wonder is how he can maintain a balance on it at all. Yet this seems to be no part of the difficulty in navigating; on the contrary, every effort of the rider seems bent on driving it at break-neck speed. The ease and celerity with which this new method of propulsion was turned around the corners of the building was amusing, and its performance was in the highest degree satisfactory."

The figures credited to the winner of each game were the first amateur records ever claimed in America, and became necessarily our bests on record.

They were a fair test of our ability in this line, and the remarkable progress in American amateur athletic sport during the past seventeen years is clearly shown by comparing those performances of 1868 with our present records. The comparison, or rather the contrast, is as follows :

Marvin Safe Co. **NEW YORK, PHILADELPHIA AND LONDON.**

75-Yard Run—Then, 9 sec.; now, 7 3-4.
220-Yard Run—Then, 28 sec.; now, 22 2-5.
Quarter-Mile Run—Then, 1 min. 20 sec.; now, 48 3-4.
Half-Mile Run—Then, 2 min. 26 sec.; now, 1:55 2-5.
Hurdle-Race—Then, 24 sec.; now, 16 4-5.
One-Mile Walk—Then, 7 min. 50 1-2 sec.; now, 6:29 3-5.
Standing Long Jump (with weights)—Then, 11 ft. 6 1-5 in.; now, 12 ft. 9 1-2 in.
Standing High Jump—Then, 4 ft. 5 in.; now, 5 ft. 1 1-4 in.
Three Standing Long Jumps (with weights)—Then, 33 ft. 8 in.; now, 35 ft. 9 in.
Running Long Jump—Then, 17 ft.; now, 22 ft. 7 3-4 in.
Running High Jump—Then, 5 ft. 2 in.; now, 6 ft. 1-4 in.
Pole-Leaping—Then, 8 ft. 3 in.; now, 11 ft. 1-2 in.
Throwing Hammer—Then, 73 ft.; now, 96 ft. 10 in.
Putting Shot—Then, 35 ft. 5 in.; now, 43 ft.

Of the athletes who assisted in forming the club and giving its first games, Jason H. Miller remains the oldest active member.

DECEASED MEMBERS.

J. Edward Russell, David L. S. Dorian, H. J. Magrane, Charles T. Roosevelt.

NOT NOW CONNECTED WITH THE CLUB.

Harry A. Hiers,	William J. Sleight,	H. Sanford,
W. J. Hiers,	Edward Garrison,	W. J. Wise,
P. M. Broderick,	Joseph Benson,	J. McGonigle,
F. W. Stone,	Joseph Russell,	Thomas Sturgis
A. R. S. Foote,	Matthew Arnold,	W. H. Walsh,
Frank Johnson,	P. O'Hara,	S. Wilson,
Arthur Vinette,	Edward Gleason,	J. Fuessel,
Leon Baker,	G. Wilkins,	E. B. Ketchum,
Morris E. Burton,	J. C. O'Connell,	D. W. Wise, Jr.
E. R. Edwards,	Charles S. Osborn,	

The three founders of the club—Babcock, Buermeyer and Curtis—were several years ago transferred from active to honorary membership, but are still residents of New York city and in vigorous health.

The history of the New York Athletic Club, since its first open amateur meeting, is an oft-told tale, and needs but brief recapitulation. In 1869 the parlor at 200 Sixth avenue grew too small for those who wished to enjoy its pleasures, and larger apartments were secured in Clarendon Hall. In 1870 the club was incorporated, its indoor headquarters transferred to the St. Mark's Place Gymnasium, and a small floating boat-house built and anchored near Harlem Bridge.

MARVIN'S "TONGUE and GROOVE" SAFE.

Next year its indoor rendezvous was changed to John Wood's Gymnasium, in 28th street, and the vacant lots between Third avenue, Lexington avenue, 130th street and the Harlem River, leased an changed into athletic grounds, with a sixth-of-a-mile track, and the club boat-house anchored along the back-stretch. In 1876 a large floating boat-house was built, and the two houses anchored at the foot of 138th street, Mott Haven—a spot now occupied by the approaches to the Madison avenue bridge. Next year the club obtained a long lease of the vacant plot on the north bank of the Harlem River, near 150th street, and transformed it into the beautiful grounds which it has since occupied. Soon afterward the two boat-houses were moved to the foot of the street adjoining the grounds, thus concentrating the club's athletic and aquatic interests in a most convenient and comfortable manner. In 1882 the club's indoor headquarters were removed to the Crescent Club Gymnasium, in 23d street, and in 1885 made their final journey to a permanent home in the club's magnificent house, corner of 6th avenue and 55th street.

No one can deny that the New York Athletic Club is the leading amateur athletic organization of the United States. It has invested in grounds, boat-houses and club-houses more money than any other American club. It was the first and is the largest amateur club in the country; and as regards social, financial and athletic standing, its members compare favorably with those of any club in the world. For these reasons, it is eminently fit and proper that the New York Athletic Club should take the lead in developing and promoting amateur athletic sports in America, and the duties thus thrust upon the club by its character and standing have been performed with unusual intelligence, tireless enterprise, strict impartiality and becoming modesty.

During its early years the history of the New York Athletic Club was in fact, the history of American amateur athletic sports; and, even after a hundred sister clubs had been formed, the worthy deeds of the pioneer club still enriched every page of our athletic annals. It has been constantly "foremost in every good athletic word and work;" prompt to investigate every invention and adopt every improvement; persistently active and earnest in developing and improving amateur athletic sport. It made athletic sports popular and respectable, and rendered it possible that amateur athletic clubs should exist and flourish. Its object, as expressed in its charter, was not the building up and aggrandizement of the New York Athletic Club, but the development and progress of amateur athletic sports in America; and it has neither unseemly pride in its own members nor unmanly jealousy of its neighbors.

MARVIN'S SAFE CANNOT BE TAKEN APART WITH A COMMON SCREW DRIVER.

It gave the first open amateur meeting ever held in America. It imported the first spiked shoes ever worn by an American amateur, and introduced to this country the style of athletic costume which is now universally adopted. It built and owned the first athletic grounds, and constructed the first cinder running-path ever seen in the United States. It introduced handicapping, and gave the first handicap games ever known here. It gave the first tug-of-war and the first steeplechase, and was ever alert to introduce any novelty that had merit. It perfected the machinery of its own management until its constitution, by-laws and general rules were in constant demand for the guidance of new clubs, and revised, improved and codified the rules governing competitions with such intelligent skill that its laws of athletics and rules for the government of athletic meetings, were subsequently adopted by the National Association without alteration or amendment.

In 1876, by the advice and with the consent of every amateur athletic club in this country, the New York Athletic Club gave the first annual American amateur championship athletic meeting, and continued it yearly until in 1879 it gracefully transferred this duty to the newly-formed Amateur Athletic Association. In 1877 it founded the annual meeting for the decision of the amateur swimming championship, and in 1878 the annual meeting for the decision of the amateur boxing and wrestling championships, and still maintains both these yearly contests.

No club in the world ever more fairly earned the right to inscribe on its banner that manly motto: "*Nulla Vestigia Retrorsum.*"

The founders of the New York Athletic Club in 1866 were very hopeful, but their most sanguine speculations hardly pictured the reality of to-day. The three members have increased to two thousand—the limit—and three hundred applicants stand waiting for the first vacancy. It has the beautiful grounds at Mott Haven, and just over the fence, on the river bank, are moored its four large boat-houses, filled with a stock of racing and pleasure boats unsurpassed in quality or number by the fleet of any American club. At the corner of Sixth avenue and Fifty-fifth street it has its own magnificent house, which includes not only a grand gymnasum and spacious swimming-bath, but also all the various comforts and conveniences of a first-class social club.

The history of the club has not been wholly free from the unpleasant incidents usual in similar organizations, but it has safely weathered the storms of outside jealousy and internal dissension, and is now snugly anchored in the harbor of assured success.

MARVIN'S FIRE & BURGLAR **SAFES.**

The officers of some of the earlier years were as follows:—

1879.

PRESIDENT:
CHARLES E. PIERCE.

VICE-PRESIDENT: TREASURER: SECRETARY:
JOHN WHIPPLE. ALFRED HEYN. C. A. MAHONEY.

CAPTAIN:
WALDO SPRAGUE.

FIRST LIEUTENANT: SECOND LIEUTENANT:
FRANK J. KILPATRICK. BENJAMIN C. WILLIAMS.

TRUSTEES:
CHARLES R. TRUAX, HENRY C. WEST,
R. WILLIAM RATHBORNE.

1880.

PRESIDENT:
WILLIAM B. CURTIS.

VICE-PRESIDENT: TREASURER:
WALDO SPRAGUE. WILLIAM M. ANDRUS.

SECRETARY:
CORNELIUS A. MAHONEY.

CAPTAIN:
ALFRED H. CURTIS.

FIRST LIEUTENANT: SECOND LIEUTENANT:
WILLIAM WOOD. WILLIAM G. DEMAREST.

TRUSTEES:
JAMES R. CURRAN, JAMES W. CARTER,
THOMAS R. KEATOR.

MARVIN'S "FORGED ANGLE FRAME" **SAFE.**

1881.

PRESIDENT:
WILLIAM B. CURTIS.

VICE-PRESIDENT:
WALDO SPRAGUE.

SECRETARY-TREASURER:
WILLIAM WOOD.

CAPTAIN:
ALFRED H. CURTIS.

FIRST LIEUTENANT:
JAMES W. CARTER.

SECOND LIEUTENANT:
GEORGE D. PHILLIPS.

TRUSTEES:

CHARLES E. PIERCE,
CHARLES B. WAITE,
WILLIAM M. ANDRUS,
BENJ. C. WILLIAMS,
THOMAS R. KEATOR,
OTTO SARONY,
JAMES R. CURRAN,
REGINALD H. SAYRE,
THEODOR GUERRA.

1882.

PRESIDENT:
WILLIAM R. TRAVERS.

VICE-PRESIDENT:
ALFRED H. CURTIS.

SECRETARY-TREASURER:
WILLIAM WOOD.

CAPTAIN:
JAS. ROSS CURRAN.

FIRST LIEUTENANT:
J. W. CARTER.

SECOND LIEUTENANT:
OTTO SARONY.

TRUSTEES:

HERMANN OELRICHS,
B. C. WILLIAMS,
T. R. KEATOR,
W. M. ANDRUS,
WILLIAM C. WILMER,
W. S. WILSON,
A. B. WILSON,
R. H. SAYRE,
F. A. BUCKMAN.

MARVIN'S SAFES Have "Recessed Door with Book Case Protector."

Among its many prominent and retired athletes may be mentioned the names of :—

Otto Sarony,	W. Hamilton,	M. W. Ford,
H. E. Buermeyer,	Geo. Phillips,	C. A. J. Quackberner,
F. Phinney,	A. B. Wilson,	D. M. Stern,
F. Jenkins,	S. Wainwright,	M. G. Morse,
J. Carter,	Geo. H. Taylor,	W. B. Curtis,
H. Barnes,	J. C. Babcock,	Frank Ellison,
Wm. Wood,	H. M. Raborg,	W. Weaver,
B. C. Williams,	F. G. Bourne,	W. C. Wilmer,
H. Goffe,	R. H. Dudgeon,	Waldo Sprague.

Following are the officers for the year 1885 :—

PRESIDENT :
WILLIAM R. TRAVERS.

VICE-PRESIDENT :
A. V. DE GOICOURIA.

SECRETARY :
ALBERT H. WHEELER.

CAPTAIN :
WALTER G. SCHUYLER.

TREASURER :
WILLIAM WOOD.

BOARD OF TRUSTEES :

SETH B. FRENCH,
JOHN J. McCOOK,
OTTO SARONY,
JENNINGS S. COX,
JOS. J, O'DONOHUE,

THOMAS R. KEATOR,
CHAS. E. QUINCEY,
RUTGERS VAN BRUNT,
EDWARD S. INNET,
WALTER STANTON.

INSTANTANEOUS
PORTRAIT & LANDSCAPE
𝔓hotographer,

TOMPKINSVILLE,

J. Almstaedt

STATEN ISLAND.

PUBLISHER OF

PHOTOGRAPHS

——OF——

STATEN ISLAND SCENERY.

Telephone Call, 48 D.

HISTORY OF THE
Staten Island Athletic Club.

WEST NEW BRIGHTON.

THE history and record of the Staten Island Athletic Club is one that should place it in the lead of the many large athletic and rowing organizations of this country, not only for its strength as an athletic and boating club, but also for its management, which has been successfully conducted on first-class business principles for the past eight years, and so much so that the members are now enabled to say that their club is entirely free from debt of any kind, while the property is valued at from $25,000 to $30,000.

The idea of starting an athletic club on Staten Island was first thought of in 1877, by an old athlete named Wm. Iken. He proposed his scheme to Messrs. Oliver T. Johnson, Robt. T. P. Fiske, Fred and Frank Janssen, John W. Edwards and W. J. U. Roberts, one morning, on the way to the city, on the North Shore ferry-boat, and the idea was cordially supported by all of the parties spoken to.

Mr. Johnson, an old reliable in sports, won the first handicap race ever run in this country; Mr. Edwards had been captain of the famous and renowned Neptune Rowing Association for several years; Mr. Roberts was one of the champion Columbia College Foot-Ball Team, while the Janssen Brothers and Mr. Fiske were members and founders of the old Alpha Base-Ball Club, well known for having won more games in six successive years (1870 to 1877) than any other amateur club in America.

These gentlemen soon took steps toward organizing a club, and not long after the matter was first proposed a meeting was called for and held in a boat-house, known at that time as the Hesper Boat Club, by thirteen enthusiastic admirers of sports in general, namely :

Wm. Iken,	Fred. W. Janssen,
Oliver T. Johnson,	Robt. T. P. Fiske,
John W. Edwards,	John H. Rimmer,
Wm. R. Wemple,	Frank G. Janssen,
Frank L. Russ,	Fred. L. Rodewald,
Wm. J. U. Roberts,	Thos. Chute,

Henry A. Caesar.

MARVIN'S "TONGUE & GROOVE" SAFE.

Seated around a little lamp, that burned dimly on the floor, these seemingly unlucky thirteen men, and already quite distinguished athletes, had but time to organize before the lamp flickered and went out, thus compelling an adjournment at the very beginning.

However, this did not discourage the men, as a second meeting was called for at the Village Hall, New Brighton, and to which each one of the thirteen gentlemen brought one or two of their friends. This time quite a meeting was held, Mr. W. K. Soutter, the banker, was elected president, by-laws and rules established, members elected, and a little supper served in remembrance. All this took place in the fall of 1877, and it was the same year that a large wagon was to be seen, with all these gentlemen inside, driving through the mud and rain down to the New Dorp Trotting Track, early Thanksgiving Day morning. Mr. Plummer, the world-renowned critic and official, was rescued from a plowed corn-field near Britton's Pond, soaked to the skin and entirely exhausted, it taking the combined efforts of the S. I. A. C. to extricate this little big sportsman from his unfortunate position.

The destination was reached in a little less than three hours, and after a little drying a number of the party stripped for some races around the half-mile track, while others were employed looking after dinner and informing Mr. Plummer of the so-far success of the club.

After some three or four races had taken place—having been run in dancing pumps, bathing-suits, and even less—the men all felt quite broken-hearted because they had not beaten the records, but each and every one thought himself the coming champion—with a little practice; and so it was owing to the untiring pluck of Iken, Johnson, Janssen, Fiske, Roberts and Rimmer that the racing was kept up, as these men could be seen daily running on the streets, in yards, and across country, on Sundays. Meanwhile the other members were doing good work toward providing a suitable track and grounds, and which was finally leased, corner of Bement and Henderson avenues.

The field had to be leveled, the track dug out and the surroundings improved. Mr. Robt. J. Wardlaw, a member, then at the School of Mines, Columbia College, undertook the job, and after some hard work made the place quite picturesque in the way of a race-track. Late in the spring of 1878 the club attempted to hold a field meeting, with the aid of a large tent in the center of the grounds as a grand stand, but owing to the rain-storm, which suddenly broke forth, but one race took place, which Wardlaw won, with Janssen second, and it was at this meeting that all the ladies, horses, carriages, carts, laborers and athletes could be seen in one body under this circus tent of A. Z. Ross.

MARVIN'S SAFE CANNOT BE TAKEN APART WITH A COMMON SCREW DRIVER.

1878.

The officers were as follows:—

PRESIDENT,
WILLIAM K. SOUTTER.

REC. SECRETARY,	TREASURER,	COR. SECRETARY,
D. J. H. WILLCOX.	H. A. CAESAR.	R. T. P. FISKE.

CAPTAIN,
O. T. JOHNSON.

FIRST LIEUTENANT,	SECOND LIEUTENANT,
C. THORP.	D. H. ROWLAND.

TRUSTEES.

JOHN D. VERMEULE.	D. R. NORVELL.
JOHN W. EDWARDS.	ARTHUR T. SHAND.
LOUIS HENDERSON.	F. L. RODEWALD.

However, it was only about a month later when July 4th came, the still energetic members had another programme arranged for their many friends and admirers, who seemed to fully appreciate the combined efforts of the gentlemen engaged in the management, and so did not allow weather or climate to prevent their presence at the meeting. After two or three races had taken place, in which such men as Shand, Chute, Collins, Rodewald, Bailey and Dedrichsen could be seen striving for laurels and glory, the rain again came down in torrents, and another postponement was necessary, but only for a few days this time, as Mr. Johnson in a very eloquent speech informed the spectators that the meeting would take place on the 6th inst., two days following, while the crowd received the announcement with great applause, although the greater number were drenched through and through by this time.

Not until the Fall of 1878 did the club hold its first successful games, open to all amateurs. A grand-stand of planks and beams had been built for the occasion, and the never-tiring members, Johnson, Chute, Collins, Hayward, Wemple, Dedrechsen, Shand and Charles F. True could be seen with their hats, coats, vests, collars and cuffs all off, working like laborers, with the sun's rays pouring down upon them at an angle of 105 degrees in the shade, stretching an old lighter's mainsail over the top of the so-called grand-stand, to keep the fair sex from being burnt brown. But the games proved a success, and the club was greatly benefitted by them, while during the winter months plans and arrangements were being made for the fol-

---

MARVIN'S SAFES HAVE THE **"Sliding Back Plate."**

lowing year's work as well as a minstrel show that was gotten up and held at Odd Fellows' Hall, West New Brighton, although owing to heavy expenses, and a rather threatening night, the club made very little by the performance, the net sum being in the neighborhood of $50.

It kept the interest up in the club, however, and people were now beginning to see the S. I. A. C. gradually looming up toward a strong and large organization.

1879.

The officers were as follows:—

PRESIDENT,
W. K. SOUTTER.

VICE-PRESIDENT,	TREASURER,	SECRETARY,
D. J. H. WILLCOX.	W. A. COLLINS, Jr.	H. W. J. TELFAIR.

CORRESPONDING SECRETARY,	CAPTAIN,
R. P. G. BUCKLIN.	O. T. JOHNSON

TRUSTEES,
A. L. FARIS.   THOS. CHUTE.   J. H. RIMMER.   H. A. CAESAR.

The year 1879 passed off rather quietly, although three meetings were held, as well as some private club events. The 100 yards "Soutter" medal, and the 440 yards "Sacks" medal being then on the programme for club members. The first competition for these medals took place in 1878, at the Fall Meeting, and early in the Spring of '79 members were in training to win the handsome trophies. At first De Garmendia and Rimmer won them respectively in 10 2-5 and 56¼ seconds, while later on the former went through the hands of Roberts three times, Beers once, Janssen three times, Fiske once, Morris once, and Rimmer five times, who finally retained the prize. The fastest races were the first and last, 10 2-5 and 10½ seconds by De Garmendia and Rimmer, while the "Sacks" medal was given up by Rimmer to Janssen, who walked over, but afterwards defeated Price, Telfair, Fiske, Morris and Stursberg, running twice in 55¾ seconds. Mr. Telfair also won this medal twice before it became Janssen's personal property.

This same year many medals were brought home from outside meetings by Rimmer, Rowland, Roberts, Taylor, Iken, Johnson and Janssen, but the winter broke in rather suddenly upon the grounds, and the fast dirt track, dressing rooms, etc., were left in pretty good

Marvin Safe Co. NEW YORK, PHILADELPHIA AND LONDON.

shape. The Club being then somewhat reduced in funds, having but 63 members, it was decided to give another minstrel entertainment, this time to be held at the Lyceum, New Brighton. After working for months, the show took place, and to the great satisfaction of the audience, for it was at this performance that Messrs. Pinchback, Johnson, Charles Bramhall, Smith, Kobby, Rushmore Wood and Ralph Newton made hits such as are seldom seen at amateur entertainments; and it was owing to the limited size of the hall that more than about $100 was not cleared.

This was good work though, and when Spring made its appearance, the club had won many new friends by keeping its name in prominence, and was well prepared for the coming season's work and outlay.

1880.

The officers were as follows:—

PRESIDENT,
W. K. SOUTTER.

VICE-PRESIDENT,   TREASURER,   SECRETARY,
D. J. H. WILLCOX.   H. W. J. TELFAIR.   W. C. DAVIS.

CAPTAIN,
O. T. JOHNSON.

FIRST LIEUTENANT,   SECOND LIEUTENANT,
G. M. L. SACKS.   FRANK G. JANSSEN.

Early in April the athletes got to work and could be seen daily running upon the track, while many victories had already been won before the month of May was recorded. Fred Janssen beat the record for 1-6 of a mile hurdle at Elizabeth on May 8th by one second. Rimmer was considered one of the fastest ¼ mile runners; Roberts ran a half mile in 2.08 at the Scottish-American A. C. Games; A. L. Carroll won the championship high jump in the Fall with 5 ft. 5 in.; Beers won the high jump and hurdle race at the Canadian championship meeting, and Janssen also defeated J. E. Haigh, who was then champion, in a 220 yards hurdle race at Mott Haven. This was a match race resulting from a race at the Scottish-American A. C. Games, in which the four champions, Moritz, Janssen, Servatious and Haigh were all running to lower the American record, and after five trials, in which all four finished within a yard of each other every time, the race was given to Moritz, with Haigh and Janssen a dead heat for second.

MARVIN'S "FORGED ANGLE FRAME" **SAFE.**

At the match race Janssen won by five yards and lowered the record to 29½ seconds. Rimmer won a grand race at Short Hills, defeating Value, Inman, Reynolds and L. A. Stewart for the quarter-mile race, covering the distance in 54¼ seconds.

This was the year that Roberts, Janssen, Rimmer and Beers brought over 100 medals home to their club, they having carried the S. I. A. C. colors to the front at almost every meeting held.

Now, many of the Athletic members also belonged to one of the two boat clubs known as the Neptune and Hesper rowing clubs, so a consolidation was proposed, and after long discussion and many objections had been overcome, it was approved of, and all the members of the three clubs joined and set to work to build a boat-house by raising funds on "scrip" issued at $10 a share, bearing 6 per cent. interest and to run five years. Some $5,000 was raised in a few weeks, and it was owing to Mr. G. M. L. Sack's hard work and push that a second story was approved of and added to the plans, to be used for meetings, club-rooms, etc., etc.

Another minstrel entertainment was given in January, 1881, at Parabola Hall, New Brighton, and some $150 realized. This time, John Edwards, C. M. Johnson and R. Newton carrying off the honors of the evening.

1881.

Club officers were as follows :—

PRESIDENT,
WILLIAM K. SOUTTER.

VICE-PRESIDENT,   SECRETARY,   TREASURER,
DAVID J. H. WILCOX.   WM. C. DAVIS.   H. W. J. TELFAIR.

CAPTAIN,
JOHN W. EDWARDS.

FIRST LIEUTENANT,   SECOND LIEUTENANT,
W. G. DEDRICHSEN.   J. H. RIMMER,

The new boat house was started in the Fall of 1880, and was finished far enough for habitation the following season, so the club moved what few boats, etc. it had to its new quarters and thus boating was added to the already many attractions of this club.

This fine house started a boom in the membership, as the roll soon ran up to 260, while a year ago but 67 names were enrolled in all.

The many athletes kept up their work well and won any number of prizes, too numerous to mention, among them A. L. Carroll beat the high jump record at Philadelphia, clearing the bar at 5 feet 8 inches, and also tied with C. W. Durand at the championship meeting

MARVIN'S "TONGUE & GROOVE" SAFE.

same height, but in jumping off, Durand was in better condition and won the medal and championship with 5 feet 8 inches. Fred Janssen beat the record for the 120-yards hurdle race at Montclair, and also the one-sixth of a mile hurdle, which was already his own, at the Staten Island championships held July 4th, time being 39 3 8 seconds. J. H. Rimmer won the 220-yards "Soutter" challenge medal and also the one-half mile "Starin" medal which cost $185, and was presented to the club by Hon. John H. Starin. Rimmer's fastest time was 2.09¼ seconds.

Messrs. J. H. Hayward and Lewis Morris presented medals to be rowed for in single sculls, the former being won three times by W. C. Rowland, and the latter became W. J. M. Roberts' property, he having won it three times in accordance with the conditions.

A medal for swimming was given by Mr. Charles A. White, distance one-half mile, and to become the property of the member winning it best two in three races. Roberts won the first race and C. Ed. Dejonge the second and third and medal with apparent ease.

This year a Lacrosse team was sent to the New Jersey State Fair at Waverley, N. J., and after some hard fighting succeeded in capturing a set of colors as the second prize. The work of Magee, Telfair, the Janssen Brothers and Roberts being worthy of note. The same team also played at Bay Ridge against the Brooklyn team and came out victorious after a rough and tumble fight over hills, stones, bushes and trees. Mr. White distinguished himself in this game by laying the cheek and eye of the captain of the Brooklyn team open with a cut four inches long from a blow on the head during a scrimmage near the goal.

The members were now rowing as well as running, and the many clubs along the beautiful Kills had formed an Association known as the Kill Von Kull Rowing Association.

This started in 1879, and among some of the races won by this club may be mentioned the four-oared shell, four-oared barge, pair-oared shell and single sculls. The fours by W. G. Dedrichsen, C. A. White, R. T. P. Fiske and W. C. Rowland in 1880, and W. G. Dedrichsen, W. M. Christopher, C. A. White and Fiske in 1881. Barge by Cadmus, Van Zandt, Caesar and Conroy, with Edwards, coxs'n., and the pairs by Roberts and Telfair.

The former shell crew also won the Harlem River race for four-oared shells in 1880.

Of course many races were also lost, and the boys were often made to take a back seat both on land and water, for although good men, they could not expect to get along much faster than they were going. They were young as well as the club, but with the

MARVIN'S SAFES Have "Recessed Door with Book Case Protector."

pluck and untiring hearts of would-be fame, they were fast making names in the athletic world of this country, both for themselves and the Staten Island Athletic Club.

By this time the boat-house looked very handsome from the outside, but the interior was quite unfinished, and the building, together with board fences, houses, large dressing rooms, and grandstands on the athletic grounds had pretty well used up the funds of the club, so it was decided to let the interior remain unfinished for the present, when at a late meeting Mr. F. W. Janssen proposed holding a Fair, the proceeds of which were to be applied to fitting up the inside of the house and finishing it off with hard wood.

After a greet deal of objecting, a motion to hold the Fair was carried by a small majority., and Messrs. Janssen, Rowland, Carroll and Davis were appointed a committee of four as managers, after Messrs. Soutter, Janssen, Johnson and Chute had guaranteed the club against loss in case the Fair was not a success.

Work went on slowly, but in earnest, and after many drawbacks and seemingly impossible obstructions had been overcome, the doors of the Young Men's Christian Association, at West New Brighton, were thrown open to the public on December 12th, and remained so for three evenings only. The different tables were matronized by the lady friends of the members, while each matron had three young lady assistants. Mr. "R. Penn Smith, Jr.," with his assistant "Kelly" managed to beat the public out of $21.37 by managing the shooting gallery. A Life Membership to the club was raffled among members at $1 a chance, and brought $165, being $65 over and above the original value.

The following articles were voted for at ten cents a vote, and afterwards presented to the party or club receiving the highest number of votes:—

    Fire Trumpet brought $ 8.50 to Zephyr Hose Co.
    Fire Screen " 87.40 to Mrs. E. W. Gould.
    Barge Colors " 7.50 to S. I. A. C.
    Gold Medal " 93.70 to Mr. F. W. Janssen.
    Fishing Rod " 59.80 to Mr. B. S. Beckwith.

The weather was something fearful every night, and but fifty members were present to do justice to the club, but owing to the ladies endeavors and influence, the total receipts for the three evenings amounted to $1,350, which gave the club a net balance of $975.

This sum was all sunk in the second-story of the Boat House, mostly in panelling the main room with hard wood. This same year three more challenge medals presented by Messrs. W. R. White, .W

Marvin Safe Co. NEW YORK, PHILADELPHIA AND LONDON.

K. Soutter, and Bartens and Rice, 1 mile run, ¼ mile run and one mile walk respectively, became the personal property of C. E. Dejonge, J. J. Hoff and H. W. Janssen, they being the successful athletes at the respective distances.

The Sacks' Diamond Medal, made by Bartens and Rice, and costing $275, was also won and presented to J. H. Rimmer, for having scored the highest number of points during one year's racing. The leading scores being,

J. H. Rimmer,	116.
F. W. Janssen,	109.
W. J. U. Roberts,	94.

This year closed with a large balance in the treasury, and the members longing for the warm sunshine of Spring, 1882.

The year opened with the Spring games on May 10th, and which were the most successful ever giving by this Club, as the gate receipts amounted to between $500 and $600, while every one present enjoyed the great crowd and good racing.

The Club gave three Field Meetings as usual, while most of the running for the home Club was done by Hoff, Harry Janssen, C. E. Dejonge, DeMacarty, Carroll and Meeker, the other older athletes having won their 50 to 100 medals apiece, and retired on their laurels. A. L. Carroll again won the Championship High Jump of America, with 5 ft. 7 in., and also the Championship of Canada, with 5 ft. 8in. Many other less important events were won, the "Black and Yellow" being carried to the front by Hoff, Janssen, C. A. White and A. B. Rich.

In June came the 2nd annual Club Regatta, held off the Boat House, and following is a list of events and winners:—

Pair-oared Shell:
Roberts and Telfair, 1st.
White and Rowland, 2nd.

Senior Single:
Rowland, 1st.
Fiske, 2nd.

Four-oared Shell:
F. W. Janssen, Bow.
H. W. Janssen, 2.
H. B. Rich, 3.
A. L. Carroll, Stroke.

Defeated:
F. G. Janssen, Bow.
H. W. J. Telfair, 2.
W. J. U. Roberts, 3.
C. A. White, Stroke.

R. T. P. Fiske, Bow.
W. C. Rowland, 2.
W. M. Christopher, 3.
W. G. Dedrichsen, Stroke.

MARVIN'S ARE THE BEST **SAFES.**

The Pair-oared Gig was won by Baker and Hoff, with Ellis, Coxs'n.

In the Junior Single, Harry Janssen defeated W. Y. Wemple, while the Four-oared Barge was won by,

>R. T. P. Fiske,
>R. P. G. Bucklin,
>Wm. M. Christopher,
>Wm. G. Dedrichsen,
>J. W. Magee, Coxs'n.

Rodewald and F. G. Janssen beat Edwards and Jewett in the Double Scull Race and the Eight-oared Shell resulted in an easy thing for Fiske's crew. In the evening there was a reception and dance in the Boat House at which the fair sex from New Brighton, with a number from New York, were present, and the whole affair terminated as a perfect success on both land and water.

In 1883, the Kill Von Kull Association, composed of the Staten Island Athletic, Arthur Kull Boat and Alcyone Rowing Clubs, and the Viking, Bayonne and Argonanta Rowing Associations, held its 4th Annual Regatta at Elizabethport, and of the 5 events in which the S. I. A. C. started, but one was won owing to lack of interest and training among the old athletes. Roberts captured the Senior Single with Rowland 2nd.

The Club held its Third Annual Regatta off the Club House, as usual, and the races were close, exciting, and well contested from start to finish. In the Junior Single Scull, Edgar Hicks defeated H. S. Redmond and J. W. Magee, while Harry Janssen made the old veteran Roberts succumb in grand style in the race for the Seniors. After the Eight-oared Shell Race was over, but little time was lost before the reception took place. This was given at the Club House as usual in the evening, and was a most delightful and successful affair, the Island's beauty and fashion being fully represented. Some 450 people were present; the music was unusually fine; the supper of marked excellence, and all entered into the enjoyment of the dancing most heartily. During the evening the prizes to the winners of the Regatta, consisting of silver cups, were awarded by the President, Oliver T. Johnson, amidst much applause.

In the Fall, challenge medals for quarter and half-mile runs, presented by Mr. O. T. Johnson and Mr. J. E. Faber, were won by C. E. Taylor and C. E. Dejonge respectively.

MARVIN'S FIRE & BURGLAR **SAFES.**

THE STATEN ISLAND ATHLETIC CLUB.

Following were the officers for this year:—

PRESIDENT,
O. T. JOHNSON.

VICE-PRESIDENT, SECRETARY, TREASURER,
H. O. BAILEY. W. C. DAVIS. F. W. JANSSEN.

CAPTAIN,
F. L. RODEWALD.

FIRST LIEUTENANT, SECOND LIEUTENANT,
H. B. RICH. H. W. JANSSEN.

TRUSTEES,

O T. JOHNSON,	F. W. JANSSEN,
W. C. DAVIS,	F. L RODEWALD,
H. W. J. TELFAIR,	A. L. FARIS,
W. F. DISOSWAY,	JOS. W. BOYLE.
JOHN W. EDWARDS,	J. E. FABER.

Nearly all the first half of the winter the members could be found busy rehearsing and preparing for a mammoth minstrel entertainment under the management of Messrs. F. W. Janssen, L. B. Frieze, Jr., J. W. Edwards and W. C. Davis. The performance was given at the German Club Rooms at Stapleton, S. I., on January 12th, 1884, and was a most brilliant affair throughout, the ladies and gentlemen being in full dress without an exception, the hall crowded to the doors, and the whole entertainment of unusually fine character.

Shortly before eight o'clock, a colored gentleman, wearing a linen duster and carrying an old umbrella, an American flag and a bundle of sheet music, was escorted by an usher down the centre aisle of the hall. As he advanced towards the orchestra, the colored gentleman displayed on his back a card which read:—

"*N. Y. HERALD.*
"D. H."

The colored citizen was Prof. H. J. Tyndale, leader of the orchestra, and who had in store for the audience a treat in the shape of an original musical production entitled "Frisky Fiddler Polka," played on this occasion for the first time. When the curtain arose on the first, or olio portion of the entertainment, a semi-circle of seventeen

Marvin Safe Co. NEW YORK, PHILADELPHIA AND LONDON.

performers, dressed in the orthodox scissor-tailed coats and immaculate shirt bosoms, made their bow and opened the fun of the evening. On C. M. Johnson and J. W. Edwards developed the duties of endmen, while Oliver T. Johnson presided as middle-man. Some fine ballads and comic songs, winding up with the great circus act comprised the first part, and the curtain went down in deafening applause. In the second part, Mr. Frank Wilson gave a budget of droll speeches, Mr. William Mulhall an exhibition of clog and fancy dancing, Messrs. Newton and Roehner an excellent song and dance sketch, Mr. Frank C. Bowen kept the audience laughing for half an hour trying to explain an astronomical problem, Messrs. Pinchback and Johnson gave some very elegant banjo duetts, and the whole concluded with the Charleston Blues drill by the following S. I. A. C. members:—

W. C. Davis, *Capt.*
F. W. Janssen, *Lieut.*

F. C. Miller.	W. Miller.
E. Hicks.	W. B. Glassford.
Harry Van Vechten.	S. D. Palmer.
B. J. Carroll	W. Y. Wemple.
A. L. Carroll.	W. B. Farrar.
H. U. Jackson.	L. B. Frieze, Jr.
W. C. Rowland.	H. Van Vechten.
I. Almstaedt,	J. D. Vonhoevenburg.

Now the athletes were beginning to tire of the track and grounds, while such a fine club house, good bathing and sociable surroundings were much nearer, and being offered so many more and less fatigueing inducements in the way of athletic exercises, than going to the track to run, took advantage of them, and therefore did not give a sufficient amount of time to the track duties, and the consequences were that but little work was done outside of a few men. The Junior Four-oared Shell crew did good work during the summer, as on Decoration Day they won their heat at the Passaic Regatta, defeating crews from the Triton and Institute Clubs, and came in second to the Passaics in the final, after a splendid race, losing by less than a length, and defeating the Princetons, Institutes and Tritons, while a week later at the Harlem Regatta, with such competitors as the Atalantas, Nassaus and Metropolitans, they covered themselves with glory by winning the race in 6 min. 28 sec. Unfortunately at the Kill Von Kull Regatta held on the 2d of September, the Four-Oared race

MARVIN'S "FORGED ANGLE FRAME" SAFE.

was started before this crew got to the starting line, or the result might have been changed, while as it was, the Alcyone crew crossed the line a winner for the first time at this event. The home club's crew was composed of Frank Janssen, bow, R. Conyngham, 2, H. B. Rich, 3, and Harry Janssen, stroke.

The Club Regatta was held on July 10th. with the following events- Junior and Senior Singles, Four-oared Barge, Gig and Shell, and Eight-oared Shell. In the Junior Single H. J. Tyndale defeated Richards, A. B. Rich, Magee and Redmond, while Harry Janssen easily beat Hicks and Roberts in the race for the Seniors. The Eight-oared Shell Race was made up of two crews, in which the Married men rowed against the Single, and after a close race for three-quarters of a mile, the Single men proved their ability to outstay the Married by one boat length. The crews were composed of—

W. G. Dedrichsen,	O. T Johnson
C. A. White,	W. J. U. Roberts,
W. A. Lentilhon,	F. L. Rodewald,
H. J. Tyndale,	J. W. Edwards,
L. Morris, Coxs'n for the Married,	

and

R. Conyngham,	W. C. Rowland,
G. Richards,	J. E. Bonner.
F. C. Miller,	H. G. Van Vechten,
Frank Janssen,	Harry Janssen.

with Fred Janssen. Coxs'n for the Singles.

The hop in the evening was one of the most brilliant events of its class ever held on Staten Island, while among the 500 people present, could be seen many of the Toronto Lacrosse Club.

At the Kills Regatta this year the club was sustained by W. C. Rowland winning the Senior Single from Annet and four others.

Much credit is due to the embryo yachtsman of this club whose fleet, consisting of some half dozen canoes, a sharpie and three jib and mainsail boats of from 14 to 20 feet in length, may be seen, wind and weather permitting, darting through the water of the Kills and Bay, showing evidence of no mean skill on the part of their captains.

In August it was decided to hold a Regatta of these small boats over a triangular course of about five miles.

Messrs. E. Hicks and P. C. Sus were appointed Judges, Captain Frank Janssen, Referee, and a "set of colors" provided for the winning boat, (having been presented by Mr. P. Ç. Sus.)

MARVIN'S "FORGED ANGLE FRAME" **SAFE.**

The date fixed was the 23d, and five of the fleet appeared at the starting point, namely:—

"Ada"............20 feet..............W. D. Wiman
'Josie"...........18 feet................L. Morris
"Oriole"..........14 feet..............L. B. Frieze, Jr.
"Surge"....... . 16 feet.............H. O. Bailey.
"Sharpie".........16 feet...............A. Jacoutot.

The start, which was a flying one, was made a little after four P. M. A brisk breeze was blowing from the S.E., and the picture made by the tiny crafts as they dashed off to their first mark was one to be remembered by those who witnessed the race.

A preparatory signal was given first, and five minutes later the signal to start was sounded.

The first boat to cross the line was the "Oriole" at 4-42-35. Three seconds later the "Josie;" "Surge" at 4-42-50, "Sharpie" next and lastly the "Ada" at 4-44-0.

With the wind abeam, the boats flew towards Robbins Reef Light.

The wind piping up a merry tune, and Mistress "Ada" dancing by all her competitors; around the Light they jibe, "Ada," "Oriole," "Josie," "Surge" and "Sharpie" in the order named. Now with booms to starboard and jibs whiskered out to port they make for Greenville Dock. "Josie" tackles "Oriole" for second place, and catching a puff of the now dying breeze, hauls round the second mark well up in the race, and begins to beat home against a flood tide.

"Oriole" and "Surge" are close on her heels, and had the wind held, the finish would have been much closer than it was.

In order to avoid the tide, "Josie" and "Surge" hug close to the Bayonne shore, while the "Oriole" stands out on the starboard tack after the "Ada," a course which proved the wisest.

Gradually the boats draw near the finish (Constable's Point) which was first reached by the "Ada" at 5.49.20; "Oriole" second at 6.2.12; "Surge," "Josie" and "Sharpie" coming in in the order named.

The "Ada" therefore made the race in 1 hour 5 min. and 20 sec., beating the "Oriole 14 min. and 17 sec., and upon returning to the boat house, Captain Wiman was presented with the colors amid the cheers of the members, and so closed the first S. I. A. C. Sail Boat Regatta, while those interested had every reason to feel encouraged for future races.

MARVIN'S FIRE & BURGLAR **SAFES.**

Although third in the race, the "Surge" has carried off honors in other events, as her trophies, now decorating the club rooms, will testify, while as a specimen of a perfectly rigged and fitted canoe, she takes a foremost place.

September 14th dawned a fine day for athletic sports, and the annual Fall Games of the Club were as successful as ever. A. B. Rich and E. W. Gould, both of the S. I. A. C., won first and second in the Bicycle Race, while Rich won the 5-mile championship at Albany a week later, his time being 17 min. 44 2-5 sec., and also the 1-mile race in 3 min. ½ sec.

Eight men started in the former race and nine in the latter. Rich took up cycling in 1880, and the same year he finished first in a 2-mile race at the Polytechnic Institute games on May 20th. He won the 2-mile race in 7.28, and the 3 miles in 12.13 at the Williamsburgh A. C. Games, defeating Fiske, the Austins and W. R. Pitman. At the American A. C. Games, held on the Polo Grounds in 1884, he finished second to W. J. Powen in 7 min. 1 sec. for two miles with twelve starters. It was at the Albany Bicycle Meet that he won the above one and five-mile races, and also the championship of America.

The winter of '84 and '85 the Charleston Blues especially distinguished themselves at the Williamsburgh A. C. Minstrel show, given at the Brooklyn Academy. The Brooklyn *Times* of December 15th saying, that any crack military organization could be put to shame by the manœuvres of the sixteen men under Captain Davis and Lieutenant Janssen. The company also performed at Griffith's Hall, Port Richmond and at Chickering Hall, New York City, in the entertainment given by the Atalanta Boat Club. Here however the "Blues" part was not as good as usual, owing to the limited space of stage, but they brought down the house a number of times, and received as hearty an applause as ever.

The following gentlemen held office this year:—

PRESIDENT.
J. W. EDWARDS.

VICE-PRESIDENT,	SECRETARY,	TREASURER,
H. O. BAILEY.	W. C. DAVIS.	F. W. JANSSEN.

CAPTAIN,
F. G. JANSSEN.

FIRST LIEUTENANT,		SECOND LIEUTENANT,
C. A. WHITE.		H. VAN VECHTEN.

TRUSTEES.

J. W. EDWARDS.	F. W. JANSSEN.
W. C. DAVIS	F. G. JANSSEN.
J. E. FABER.	W. F. DISOSWAY.
H. W. J. TELFAIR	F. L. RODEWALD.
A. L. FARIS.	O. T. JOHNSON.

MARVIN'S "TONGUE & GROOVE" SAFE.

All these years the club had been paying 6 per cent. interest on its "scrip" debt, as well as investing some $900 yearly in boats and oars alone. The track and grounds, Club and Boat Houses were all kept in first-class condition, and the club debt was being fast wiped out.

The balance not paid off fell due on July 1st, 1885, and was paid off with interest in full to date, so that the club now stands first, financially speaking, of the many clubs around this vicinity. It is entirely free of debt in every respect, while the members own all their club houses, stands, boats, etc.

In and around their large and handsome boat house may be seen 27 Single Sculls, 1 8-Oared Shell, 4 4-Oared Shells, 2 Pair Oared Shells, 3 Barges, 2 Gigs, 1 4-Oared Paper Gig, 5 Canoes, 3 Working Boats, 4 Sail Boats, 1 Steam Launch, and several other minor crafts, and all of which are in first-class condition, having been built by the well-known boat makers, Smith, of the Harlem, or Waters & Sons, of Troy. The boat house is most certainly one of, if not the finest around New York, and the members are always delighted to show their friends and visitors around at any time. The Club belongs to the National Association of Amateur Athletes, the Kill Von Kull Rowing Association, and some smaller associations unworthy of mention. The roll stands now at 270, including 18 Life Members, namely:—

W. K. SOUTTER.	ERASTUS WIMAN.
AQUILLA RICH.	OLIVER T. JOHNSON.
JOHN W. EDWARDS.	D. A. NESBITT
A. O. WILLCOX.	J. F. EMMONS.
J. R. TELFAIR.	H. G. MEEKER.
W. R. WHITE.	R. T P. FISKE.
W. WESTON.	W. L. BONES.
R. P. G BUCKLIN.	H. A. CAESAR.
E. A. ROLLINS.	

This present year has been rather quiet so far for the S. I. A. C. with one exception, owing to the weather and want of a little exertion on the part of athletes. P. J. Murphy won the hundred yards at the B. P. R. A. Games on June 17th in $10\frac{3}{4}$ sec. P. C. Worth won the 93, 220 and 440 yard runs at the 7th Regiment Games in April, the 440 at the National Guard Championships, April 7th, held at the Armory of the 13th Regiment, Brooklyn, and also the half mile at the 9th Regiment Games. Rich, the bicycle rider, is the one exception, and too much glory cannot be given to so young and magnificent a rider, as he most certainly has proven himself to be.

MARVIN SAFE CO., ESTABLISHED 47 YEARS.

Among some of his many victories may be mentioned the one and two mile races at the Citizens' Meet, held at the American Institute. The former race he won from scratch in 3.18 and the latter in 6.25. He also won the 2-mile handicap race at the Williamsburgh A. C. Games on May 30th in 6.49. On June 6th at the Yale College Games, he won the one and two mile races in 2.58 and 5.58 respectively. Then came the Kings County Wheelmen in June, at which meeting he won the 3 mile championship of America race in 9.54, and also the 2 and 10-mile races in 6.20 and 34.23 2-5, the latter being on the W. A. C. track.

He again won the championship at 4 miles later on, covering the distance in 14.02 sec. On June 20th, at the Utica Meet he won the half-mile in 1.26, and the State championship for three miles. On July 1st he took the prizes for the 1 and 3-mile races, having ridden the full distances in 3.04 and 9.54.

Mr. Aquilla B. Rich is but 20 years old, and is thought to be the coming man of this country at from one to ten miles. He is 5 ft. 5 in. high, weighs 133 pounds, and belongs also to the League of American Wheemen.

The club held a preparatory Regatta off the Boat House on June 18th for the purpose of starting the boys in, and the races were good considering the water and condition of most of the men. W. Y. Wemple won the Junior Single from Redmond and Sus, and Harry Janssen defeated Tyndale by three lengths for the Senior prize. The other races were 4-oared Barge, 4 and 8-oared Shells, the latter being a very close and exciting race throughout. The yachtsman have sailed but one race this present season so far, "Oriole," "Surge" and "Josie" contesting for a pennant presented by Mr. Morris, of the "Josie." It was the Josie's day, as with a new set of sails fully one-third larger than those of last year, she led her rivals from start to finish, and won by some 400 yards W. C. Rowland again won the Senior Single Scull Race at the Kills Regatta, defeating Messrs. Shreve and Ellsworth with comparative ease.

This record shows very plainly what the club and its members have been doing during the past eight years, while the A1 financial and social standing speaks for itself. The members are as jolly a lot as can be found anywhere, and are ready at all times to lend a helping hand to their friends and brother clubs.

The thirteen men who organized the Association have been the prime movers in all its schemes and undertakings, and they, with the help of a few others interested in the club's welfare claim, as they have a right to do, that the club is now one which will weather many heavy storms to come, and long after many brother and sister organizations have passed out of existence the "Black" and "Yellow" will be seen both on land and water as the colors of the

STATEN ISLAND ATHLETIC CLUB.

The following comprise the officers for the year ending March 1st, 1886:—

PRESIDENT,
J. W. EDWARDS.

VICE-PRESIDENT,	SECRETARY,	TREASURER,
H. O. BAILEY.	WM. C. DAVIS.	GEO. M. MACKELLAR.

CAPTAIN,
WM. C. ROWLAND.

FIRST LIEUTENANT,	SECOND LIEUTENANT,	COR SECRETARY,
W. J. U. ROBERTS.	A. B. RICH.	E. HICKS.

TRUSTEES,

J. W. EDWARDS.	W. C. DAVIS.
GEO. M. MACKELLAR.	W. C. ROWLAND.
O. T. JOHNSON.	J. E. FABER.
W. LENTILHO.	L. B. FRIEZE, Jr.
W. F. DISOSWAY.	H. W. J. TELFAIR.

The Janitor, William Hegarty, and Track Master, Jerry Mahoney, are two obliging and respectful men. The former, especially, is always on the lookout for the boys' wants, and is thought much of by the Athletes of the Club.

For several years past this club has been contemplating buying some land where an athletic track, grand stands, club house, etc., could be built in keeping with its elegant boat-house.

This piece of land has now been obtained on Bement avenue (the same street the present grounds are located on), and next year the friends, athletes and visitors of the S. I. A. C. will see the finest track and grounds in America.

The club also intends taking up Tennis, Base Ball, Foot Ball and Lacrosse in addition to their now many sports, and the members will take part in all these games, while the club intends giving matches, tournaments and such like entertainments.

MARVIN'S SAFES Have "Recessed Door with Book Case Protector."

The new grounds are 420 by 450 feet, and at present (in its rough state) the field has but 1¼ feet grade over its entire surface.

The grounds cost $10,000 cash, and have been paid for as follows : $2,500 scrip to members, bearing 5 per cent. interest per annum, and $7,500 bond and mortgage.

It is the intention of the club to hold a fair this coming winter, and in time to come this organization will undoubtedly show the world at large what a club house is and should be, while over the door will appear the letters:—

S. I. A. C.

Geo. L. Burr Co.,
FINE MERCHANT TAILORING
OF EVERY DESCRIPTION.

Warerooms: 142 Fulton St., New York.

Established 1865.

Country Order Department.

Organized 1865.

Rules for Self-measure, Samples, Price Lists and Book of Fashions,

SENT FREE

on application.

PROGRESSIVE!   PRACTICAL!   POPULAR!

The present year marks the twenty-fourth in Business and FIFTH of our

NEW DEPARTURE,

Which consists, besides having an UNLIMITED VARIETY to select from

The BEST ARTISTIC SKILL
In Workmanship.

The HIGHEST VALUE
For the Lowest Price.

In combining such ECONOMIC ADVANTAGES as to avoid the ENORMOUS EXPENSES and INEVITABLE LOSSES incident to and inseparable from prevailing systems, and enabling us to make garments TO MEASURE cheaper and very much better than even the READY-MADE.

The inestimable advantages of our System are fully and favorably recognized by thousands. Upon its merits we continue to invite your esteemed favors

———ALL KINDS OF———

ATHLETIC and PASTIME SUITS at Specially LOW PRICES.
ATHLETIC and PASTIME SUITS at Specially LOW PRICES.
ATHLETIC and PASTIME SUITS at Specially LOW PRICES.

OVER **5,000** PATTERNS

TO SELECT FROM IN

SUITINGS, OVERCOATINGS, TROUSERINGS,

OF EVERY DESCRIPTION.

IT WILL PAY YOU TO CALL AND EXAMINE.

GEO. L. BURR CO.,
142 FULTON ST., NEW YORK.

First Floor, Up-Stairs.

HISTORY OF THE
Williamsburgh Athletic Club,
BROOKLYN.

To lovers of athletic sports throughout the country the initials
"W. A. C."
have considerable significance. In Brooklyn and New York, folks who do not even know the difference between a handicap and a hurdle understand their meaning. They appear in many an official record in connection with feats accomplished by pluck, endurance and agility. And they can be found on many a trophy won on fiercely contested fields.

The Williamsburgh Athletic Club, for which it is hardly necessary to say the letters stand, is one of the institutions of Brooklyn. It has made a record unsurpassed in the same period of time by any similar organization and made the City of Churches second to none as the home of victorious athletes. While Brooklynites take a just pride in their representative club, comparatively few of them are aware from what a small beginning the organization has grown to its present powerful proportions, or the small space of time in which it has accomplished so much. Most residents have seen the spacious, finely appointed club-house and grounds on DeKalb avenue, but not many remember the first home of the club.

When clubs from which the W. A. C. have since wrested laurels were as powerful as now, the Williamsburgh Club was not even conceived. It was in January, 1879, that the project of forming an athletic organization in the Eastern District was first discussed. Three young men were the projectors, and they had no idea at the time that they were laying the corner stone of a structure that would be one of the staunchest in the land. They were in earnest, however, and in a week had interested two more youths in the scheme :

T. V. FORSTER,   C. GANBERT,
C. C. HASELTON,   JOHN WOOD, Jr.,
                T. WATSON.

MARVIN'S "TONGUE & GROOVE" SAFE.

The five started the Williamsburgh Athletic Club, and organized on January 21, 1879. It was not long before the membership roll included 50 names, and the club was incorporated on November 17th, 1879.

When this point had been reached, the new club secured a meeting room over Wright's Business College, which, while very good for a social gathering, did not give much opportunity as a training place. None of the members possessed any more wealth than the law alowed, but they all had plenty of vim and an abiding faith that the club would come out all right. Each contributed within his means towards a fund started to lease a suitable place as a club house.

By the time summer approached the fund contained enough to lease a plot of ground on the corner of Bedford avenue and Rutledge street, but there was not a great deal left in the treasury to improve the ground. That, however, did not worry the members to any great extent. Their object in forming the club was physical culture, and they realized that there was no better way of getting up muscle than by juggling earth with picks and shovels. A few laborers had been employed, but if the members had not thrown off their coats and gone to work every fine evening they would have had to wait a good while longer before the track was finished. There were twelve laps to the mile on the track thus built. A rude stand, capable of seating about 150 spectators, was constructed, and a tent was put up to serve the double purpose of a club house and dressing-room combined.

At this time the go-as-you-please contests were all the rage, and the first exhibition given by the club was a two hours go-as-you-please match with about a dozen entries. Thirteen miles and seven laps stood to the credit of the winner. During the following fall the first annual games of the club were given, when the results achieved went rather beyond expectations.

The following gentlemen were officers in 1880 and 1881:—

1880.

PRESIDENT,
WILLIAM C. BRYANT.

VICE-PRESIDENT,	TREASURER,	SECRETARY,
FRANK SPERRY.	CHAS. C. HASELTON.	JOHN WOOD, Jr.
COR. SECRETARY,		FIN. SECRETARY,
N. L LYON.		WALTER BROWER.
	CAPTAIN,	
	WALTER SMITH.	
FIRST LIEUTENANT,		SECOND LIEUTENANT,
WM. H. HANDY.		F. M. PRICE.

MARVIN'S SAFE <u>CANNOT BE TAKEN APART WITH A COMMON SCREW DRIVER.</u>

CLUB HANDICAPPER,
GILBERT C. PETERKIN.

TRUSTEES:

WILLIAM C. BRYANT.	JOHN T. ROBERTS.
N. I. LYON.	LEWIS H. SLOCUM.
JOHN WOOD, JR.	DANIEL T. GATESON.
BENJ. W. WILSON, JR.	CHARLES C. HASELTON.
THOMAS V. FORSTER.	FRANK SPERRY.
JOSEPH G. LIDDLE.	CHARLES HUSTED.

1881.

PRESIDENT,
W. D. LIDDLE.

VICE-PRESIDENT,	SECRETARY,	TREASURER,
FRANK SPERRY.	JOHN WOOD, JR.	WM. C. BRYANT.

COR. SECRETARY,	FIN. SECRETARY,
FRANK MASON.	JOSEPH G. LIDDLE.

CAPTAIN,
GEORGE A. WEBSTER.

FIRST LIEUTENANT,	SECOND LIEUTENANT,
THEO. A. CHOICENER.	ROBT. H. CLARKE.

TRUSTEES,

W. D. LIDDLE.	GEORGE A. WEBSTER.
JOHN T. ROBERTS.	JOHN WOOD, JR.
BENJ. W. WILSON, JR.	C. C. HASELTON.
WILLIAM C. BRYANT.	LEWIS H. SLOCUM.
N. I. LYON.	J. G. LIDDLE.
D. T. GATESON.	M. W. GLEASON.

Once the club was fairly established, the list of membership increased, and it was determined to secure larger quarters, which were obtained at Wythe avenue, Penn and Rutledge streets. Here a track, measuring eight laps to the mile, was laid out, a club-house and gymnasium built, and a commodious grand stand constructed. The boys were very proud when they moved into their new quarters, which were, however, insignificant compared to the elegant club-house and grounds they now occupy. A subscription was raised to purchase the necessary apparatus for the gymnasium from the members, and efforts were made to place the club among the leading athletic organizations. The annual Spring games proved that this could be accomplished.

Amateurs of prominence attended the succeeding meetings, three or four of which were given every season, and during the three years that the grounds were used many records were beaten, and not a few champions owe their progresss to practice on the track. In the Spring of 1884 it was learned that the lease of the property could not

MARVIN'S SAFES Have "Recessed Door with Book Case Protector."

be renewed, and finding that they were outgrowing the old place, a grand athletic boom was started among the members, and they secured the block on the corner of DeKalb and Classon avenues, known as the old Clohaven Estate.

This was the club's greatest effort, and to secure the property and put it into proper shape required a large outlay of money, which was obtained through the co-operation of several wealthy gentlemen.

Work was commenced in March, 1884, and by May a complete transformation had been wrought in the neglected grounds and deserted old mansion, which had the reputation of being haunted. A splendid cinder-track, measuring five laps to the mile, was laid out and the dilapidated old homestead turned into a really elegant clubhouse. Large grand and free stands were built. Besides this, a bowling alley was constructed in a separate building, and the old club-house was moved down, painted and altered to be used as a gymnasium.

So, in a short time they refitted the old mansion and built a fine track, with grand stands, having a seating capacity of 3,000. The track was laid by the veteran Jack McMasters. It has well-rounded corners, is drained well, and measures twenty feet in width.

The house of the club is not only commodious, but very complete and beautiful. It consists of the old mansion and an annex on each side.

The ladies' reception-room is on the first floor proper. It is finished exclusively in the colors of the club—blue and gold. Sumptuous furniture in blue and gold embossed plush abounds, a remarkably handsome *tete-a-tete* chair occupying the place of honor. Even the globes of the chandelier are composed of an equal number in the prevailing colors. The blue silk championship flag worn by the baseball team two years ago stands in a corner. The rear parlor is similarly adorned with a rich championship emblem captured three years ago by a quartette of athletes belonging to the club. Across the handsome hall is the reading and smoking-room. Here the "Knights of the Round Table" congregate nightly, and make the walls ring with melodious songs and witty jokes. A long and narrow table, strewn with books and periodicals, chiefly of a sporting character, is the principal object in the apartment. Rosewood chairs, finished in leather, are scattered about promiscuously. Both the parlor and reading-room extend the entire depth of the house.

The executive chambers are on the second floor. They consist of two apartments. The one is set apart for the use of the manager and the board of trustees, and the other is devoted to the use of the different committees. The mantel of the committee-room is orna-

MARVIN'S FIRE & BURGLAR **SAFES.**

mented with excellent portraits of the club's champion ball-tossers of two years ago, as also their ambitious successors of the present season. On this floor are also two rooms where cards, checkers, chess and dominoes are indulged in, to while away pleasantly the long evenings. The tables are of cherry-wood, and the chairs of the unique little pattern known as Venice. The checker-table—a pretentious piece of furniture—is composed of solid ebony.

That portion of the house most frequented by the more muscular of the members is the top floor. A suggestive-looking platform, fourteen feet square and one foot high, in the middle of the room, leaves no doubt in the mind of the visitor as to what use it is put. A gas-fixture, with a dozen jets and a large reflector hanging over all is placed directly over the centre, at an elevation of nine and a half feet. Four burners, each placed in front of a powerful reflector, are placed at each corner, so as to throw the light into the inmost recesses of the apartments. It is here that the meetings of the club are regularly held. Over 300 chairs are uniformly ranged about, which, with the room left unoccupied, affords accommodations for 500.

The large field has also received considerable attention from the omnipresent manager. He has erected commodious lockers under the grand stand for the benefit of contestants, and has also constructed a safeguard for them in one of their favorite amusements—baseball. The muscle of the players having proven sometime ago to be too strong for the height of the fences, he has placed a wire netting on either side, 50 feet high and 140 feet long.

The out-buildings, though architecturally unpretentious, are still as perfect specimens of their class as could be found. The bowling alley, in particular, is fitted up in a manner that would bring joy to the average bowler's heart. There are six alleys, each with a separate run. Settees for the players are placed in the front, while directly in front of them again are chairs and tables for the amusement of the spectators. Twenty-four burners serve to light the building sufficiently for the purposes for which it was designated. The gymnasium stands on the corner of Classon avenue. It is not fully completed yet, but the work has advanced to such a stage that a fair idea of its future appearance may be obtained at a casual glance. On entering, one enters the wash-room, where the bath is entirely surrounded by marble, with a projection of the same material several feet in height, extending about the bath, at a distance of about four feet from the same. The next compartment, known as the locker-room, is finished exclusively in narrow Georgia pine, polished to a high degree. Two tiers of lockers, with twenty more in the centre, give accommodation to 350 men, two to each locker. Each closet is fas-

---

MARVIN'S SAFE. HAVE THE "Sliding Back Plate."

tened with a miniature combination lock, every man having his own combination.

The gymnasium proper is fitted up with swinging rings, horizontal bars, vaulting poles and other athletic implements. Indian clubs, boxing gloves, dumb-bells and foils also find a resting place in this section.

The first games at the present grounds were given on Decoration Day last year, when four of the best on records were made. These records were as follows: 125 yards in 12¼ seconds, by L. E. Myers, Manhattan A. C., and M. W. Ford, New York A. C. Two mile walk in 13 minutes 48 2-5 seconds, by Frank Murray, Williamsburgh A C. Three-mile run in 15 minutes 31 4-5 seconds, and five-mile run in 26 minutes 31 seconds, by Thomas F. Delaney, Williamsburgh A. C.

The inner field is used for base-ball, lacrosse, cricket, foot-ball and other like sports, and the lovers of these games will find all the space necessary for indulgence in their favorite pastimes. There is also ample room for putting the shot, throwing the hammer, tug of war, jumping and pole vaulting, where the men of muscle can give full vent to their prowess.

When the club took a lease of the property it had a membership of 200, but so rapid has its growth been since that it now numbers 1,050 names on its rolls. So numerous are the applications for membership, that the advisibility of confining the membership to 1,200 has been discussed. While occupying so prominent a position at home, the club is far from being unrecognized abroad. Secretary Walter H. Hegeman, of the W. A. C., is the official handicapper of the National Association.

Since the club has been in existence it has brought out nine individual champions and won ten championship events, a record that no other club in America can show for the same number of years. At the annual championship meeting in 1882, this city, with one athletic club (the W. A. C.), won five individual championships against New York City, with eight clubs, of which no one club won over three. There also competed, that year, representatives from Boston, San Francisco, Philadelphia, Canada and Yale and Harvard colleges, of which Yale, Harvard and Boston each won one championship, and Philadelphia two, the latter both by the same man.

This club secured Mr. Thomas Barrington, a well-known and capable gentleman, as manager. Mr. Gilbert H. Badeau, the President has done much for the advancement of the club. Besides being president of the club, he has held the honorable position of President of the National Amateur Athletic Association for the past two

MARVIN'S SAFE CANNOT BE TAKEN APART WITH A COMMON SCREW DRIVER.

years. It was through him that the championship games were held in Williamsburgh last year, this being the first time they were ever held outside of New York City.

The club has a number of prominent athletes and champions in its large membership, among whom we may mention the following: Sam Austin, well-known as referee and timekeeper at most of the sporting events in this section; Frank P. Murray, Delaney, Smith, Hatfield, Tivey, Adams, McCausland, Tobey, Mason, Brown, McDonald and Knowles.

New features are constantly being introduced by the club, which thus maintains its reputation as a leader.

The latest innovation is a series of ladies' days. One will be given each month, when the freedom of the club house and grounds will be given the guests and an entertainment provided. The latter will be given in the large meeting room at the top of the house, where a stage has been fitted up, and there is seating room for about one thousand persons. The apartment was originally built as an observatory tower and is delightfully cool.

Vocal and instrumental music and recitations will be given by professional talent, and the grounds will be illuminated by electric light and Chinese lanterns.

There are any number of "good fellows" in the club but none are more popular than Gilbert H. Badeau, the President, and Samuel C. Austin, the Captain, both of whom deserve the distinction conferred on them by their fellows. "Jack" McMasters, the trainer, is thoroughly identified with the organization, but everybody knows Jack and that he has done his share towards conquering success, although he was at first decidedly opposed to sleeping in the "haunted" house.

Following are the officers for the year ending Dec., 1885:—

PRESIDENT,
G. H. BADEAU.

VICE-PRESIDENT,	SECRETARY,	TREASURER,
F. FISHER.	WALTER G. HEGEMAN.	JOS. G. LIDDLE.

CORRESPONDING SECRETARY,	CAPTAIN,
SAM L W. SWEZEY.	FRANK M. PRICE.

FIRST LIEUTENANT :	SECOND LIEUTENANT :
SAM L C. AUSTIN.	FRED. E. SNIDER.

MARVIN'S SAFES Have "Recessed Door with Book Case Protector."

THE WILLIAMSBURGH ATHLETIC CLUB.

BOARD OF TRUSTEES :

G. H. BADEAU.
W. G. HEGEMAN.
F. M. PRICE.
F. E. CLARK.
E. H. TRECARTIN.
FRANK COLEMAN.

FRED. FISHER.
JOS. G. LIDDLE.
G. McNAUGHTON, M.D.
G. R. SMITH.
J. A. WORKS.
W. C. BRYANT.

Among the prominent American athletes, we mention the name of F. P. Murray as one of the Williamburgh Athletic Club's many champions, and following is a short record of his earlier athletic days:—

"Frank P. Murray, of the Williamsburgh Athletic Club, the amateur champion of America, is 29 years old, 5 feet 8½ inches in height, and weighs 140 pounds. For several years Murray was not very prominent in athletic circles, and it was not until 1883 that he assumed the position he now holds. In that year the walking records were absolutely at his mercy. His record for one mile (6 minutes and 29 3-5 seconds), made at the fall games of the New York Athletic Club, on a heavy track—the day being cold and damp—is certainly his finest performance. His next great record was made at the Manhattan Athletic Club grounds on November 6, 1883. Here he walked three miles against time, winning in the wonderful time of 21 minutes and 9 1-5 seconds, surpassing the record of 21 minutes and 42 2-5 seconds, made by T. H. Armstrong, Jr., September 14, 1878, and which had before appeared impregnable. On this occasion Murray also equaled his own best-on-record time for two miles—13 minutes and 59 seconds—and could have gained a new record had he been informed of his opportunity in time.

"That Murray in England—'the home of athletes'—showed the fairest and fastest walking ever seen in the world is certain, while his many friends feel confident that he, in time, will do what it is claimed is impossible—namely, walk a full mile, 'square heel and toe,' in 6 minutes and 25 seconds."

For some time past there has been talk that all was not well in the ranks of the well-known Williamsburgh Athletic Club.

The club was induced to remove to its new grounds by the growing need for a more commodious stand, and by the extremely good offer which was made them by one of their prominent and wealthy members. This gentleman agreed to lease the old Carhovan property, fit it up and give it to the club for one-half of their monthly initiation fee and dues. This advantageous offer was accepted, and worked very well for a time. It has been rumored lately that the club was in serious financial straits, and was about to disorganize.

Treasurer J. G. Liddle said that he did not consider the trouble

MARVIN'S ARE THE BEST **SAFES.**

in the club serious. The club will be reorganized in a month or six weeks. A circular will probably be sent to each member at an early date explaining the difficulties and calling for a meeting. One thing that has always made more or less trouble in the Williamsburgh Club ranks since the removal to its present quarters has been the very local name. This will be certain to receive attention at the coming reorganization meeting, and the club's name is almost sure to be changed to something distinctively Brooklyn. If it were possible, the club would have been called the Brooklyn Athletic Club; but it could not do that, as there is a Brooklyn Athletic Club in existence and which owes a good debt. The question of calling the new organization the Brooklyn Athletic Association will, with other suggestions, be discussed.

All the trouble has been made by a lot of "kickers," who thought that the gentleman who leased the place, and received in return but half of the receipts from only one direction, and was, so to speak, running the club in partnership with its officers, was getting entirely the best of the bargain. The "kickers" thought the club ought to run itself, and made a big muss at the time of the January election. They were badly defeated, and a ticket on which were the names only of those known to be in favor of continuing the old agreement was elected by an overwhelming majority. The "kickers" were beaten at least three to one, and for the time being utterly routed. In a short time, however, they began their old dissensions with the other club members, and succeeded finally in creating a new sentiment, and on April 1st the club leased the entire new property, with its improvements, and gave a chattel mortgage on their own property, the furniture, and so on.

This property they have just confessed judgment on, and gave up their possession of it on September 1st. This was to save the mortgagee, who is the gentleman who leased the property for the club in the first place, from taking legal steps. This gentleman is a member, and still friendly to the club, so that nothing will be done to injure it. The new club which is soon to be formed will occupy this clubhouse and grounds, and will be composed principally of old Williamsburgh Athletic Club members. The old agreement will certainly be entered into again. It was an entirely false idea that the gentleman who leased the club grounds for the club was getting anything good out of the bargain. All that he received over the rent he devoted to purchasing the property, and as he is a man of means, he would not have allowed the club to lose this place, no matter how low our receipts had fallen. All that had to be done was to give him half. The club has no debts that it cannot pay, and still has 700 members in good standing, whose $1 monthly dues are as certain as

MARVIN'S "FORGED ANGLE FRAME" SAFE.

can be, but a certain poor class of counter-jumpers were inadvertently let in. You know it is very hard to vote against a prospective member unless there is something absolutely out of the way with him. And these chaps, after paying their initiation fee and perhaps one month's dues, would then allow themselves to be "posted" for non-payment. All the trouble is not with the poorer men. The treasurer has had to post one man who was reputed to be worth $250,000, while many a young fellow working on a small salary lays by twenty-five cents a week to pay for his club and track privileges. The paying of one dollar at once he would feel sadly, but the twenty-five cents a week he doesn't mind. Two thousand five hundred dollars is now due from recalcitrant members, and if fifty per cent. of this sum is collected, Mr. Liddle says he'll be in luck. In the new organization the monthly payments will be changed to quarterly, payable in advance, and instead of allowing one month's grace to poor payers, as at present, twenty days' leeway only will be given.

Thus passes from existence a friendly, famous and renowned organization, well known to every athlete, to every athletic club both here and abroad, and to every well-wisher of sports in general, as the

WILLIAMSBURGH
  ATHLETIC
    CLUB.

MARVIN SAFE CO., ESTABLISHED 47 YEARS.

B. Spalding de Garmendia,

IMPORTER

—AND—

Commission Merchant,

55 BEAVER ST.

Sole Agent in United States

—FOR—

A. GUILLAUME & CIE.,

Talence-Bordeaux,

RED AND WHITE WINES,

COGNACS,

&C., &C.

HYGEIA HOTEL,

Old Point Comfort, Va.

100 YARDS FROM FORT MONROE.

Open all the Year. Accommodates 1,000 Guests.

Lovely Environment,
    Delightful Climate,
        Excellent Cuisine,
            Comfortable Beds,
Notable Characteristics.

Only Health and Pleasure Resort
IN AMERICA

POSSESSING

TURKISH. RUSSIAN, ROMAN, ELECTRIC, VAPOR,
MEDICATED, HOT SEA, and FRESH WATER BATHS

(Recently Instituted at a cost of $20,000.)

Terms Reasonable.

Send for Descriptive Pamphlet.

H. PHŒBUS,
Proprietor.

HISTORY OF THE
Manhattan Athletic Club.
NEW YORK CITY.

This foremost athletic organization of the United States was organized in the year 1876 and incorporated in 1877 by the following gentlemen:—

George W. Carr.
George W. Thomas.
Samuel B. Pomeroy.
Walter H. Griffin.
Robert B. Culbert.

George D. Palmley.
William C. France.
Harry P. Pike.
Edward G. Gurney.
John Fraser.

Jack Goulding was the first trainer.

When first started the number of its members was twenty, and none of its athletes were prominent. The grounds on Eighth avenue between Fifty-sixth and Fifty-seventh streets were leased, and a track eight laps to the mile laid out, which at that time was considered one of, if not the fastest, of the few that then existed.

The club was very successful in developing athletes and not long after its first days of open competition, was it before many of the fastest men of this country would make their appearance on the different cinder paths in the colors of the M. A. C. In the short space of six years it has risen to the position it now holds, that of the leading athletic club of America, while its name and the record of its members are known over the whole world.

During the year 1881, '82 and '83 the Manhattan Club, at the annual Championship Meeting, won the championship emblem, thus demonstrating its right to the title of the leading athletic club of America.

It also holds the championship up to this date, and among the 50 or 60 athletes out of its 100 odd members, there are about 25 Champions of both America and England.

The new grounds, consisting of the block extending from Eighth avenue to Ninth avenue, and from Eighty-sixth street to Eighty-seventh

MARVIN'S FIRE & BURGLAR SAFES.

street, was taken possession of in June, 1883, and are probably the finest in the world. The track has been constructed on the model of that of the London Athletic Club, and is one-quarter of a mile in circuit. In addition to this it has a 220 yards stretch on the side which is straightaway, an advantage possessed by no other track in America.

The center of the ground is drained by the most approved methods in order that the part for Baseball, Football and Lacrosse may be kept from becoming heavy or soggy. The Baseball diamond has been especially prepared, having been constructed under the supervision of a prominent player, and members may be seen any day playing upon it.

At the Ninth avenue end of the grounds two sections have been reserved for, and laid out with fine Lawn Tennis courts. Of these, one section will be completely fenced in and separated from the rest of the grounds. This part, which will contain six courts, is reserved solely for the use of ladies or ladies accompanied by gentlemen, while access to same will be through a separate entrance on the side. The other part of the Tennis grounds is not separated from the track, and contains six courts for the use of club members.

At the Eighth avenue end of the grounds is the club house, dressing rooms and grand and open stands, the stands having seating capacity for 3,500 people, roofed over, and with seats, consisting of chairs, arranged in the latest improved manner. The dressing rooms are very spacious, and contain 200 lockers. The bath rooms are stationery, with shower and needle baths attached.

Besides the officers' and executive room there is a club room, a reading room and a billiard room. The club also retained possesion of the grounds at Eighth avenue and Fifty-sixth street until this season, when the lease expired, and the ground was taken for building purposes. A gymnasium is now spoken of with great interest, and will be erected on the club grounds or in a more central location. During the winter months the grounds inside the track are flooded for skating, while the admission for members is free, the club having found this a very paying scheme at the old grounds, which saw night after night crowded beyond anticipation, but the new grounds afford ample room for all, and the pleasures derived at both the club house and rink are far beyond the ideas of one who has never been there.

It was not until 1878 that the club won a championship event, and this year Thomas H. Smith crossed the finish line a winner and Champion 1-mile runner, covering the distance in 5 min. 51¼ sec.

This made the boys work harder for the year following, and L. E. Myers, the now world-renowned champion flyer, having started in

Marvin Safe Co. NEW YORK, PHILADELPHIA AND LONDON.

his athletic career, became known to the older athletes of New York.

At the second or third meeting in which Myers ran, the veteran John Fraser noted his style of running, picked him out as a runner, took him to his house, trained and posted him from time to time, and in 1879, at the championship meeting, he won the 220, 440 and 880 yard runs with ease, time being 23 3.8, 52 2-5 and 2.01 2-5 respectively.

L. E. Myers was born in Richmond, Va., February 16th, 1858 is therefore 27 years old, and weighs in condition about 115 pounds. From his early childhood, he was quite-noted for excellence at outdoor sports, and was considered at one time a very promising base-ball player. He made his debut upon the cinder path at the games of the New York Athletic Club, on Election day, November 7th, 1878. From the 18 yards mark, won the quarter mile handicap quite easily in 55 sec. At the games of the same club held at Gilmore's Garden in the winter of '78–'79, he finished second in both the 220 yards and 440 yards handicap, being beaten in both races by men to whom he was conceding long starts. The first sensation created by him was his winning the scratch half in 2 min. 10½ sec., from a large field of "cracks" at the games given by the Scottish American Athletic Club, at Gilmore's Garden, March 1, 1879. In this race he did not part company with the field until the last lap, and then won by 50 yards. At the games of the Jersey City Athletic Club, held in May at the West Side Driving Park, won the half mile handicap easily from scratch in 2 min. 8¼ sec. His first race of very great importance was when he faced the then almost invincible Ed. Merritt, in the scratch quarter at the games of the Staten Island Athletic Club, the same spring, and to the surprise of the knowing ones ran away from Merritt in the last hundred yards, and won with something to spare, in 54 sec. Merritt however, made matters even by turning the tables on Myers the following Monday, Decoration Day, when he defeated Myers by two yards in 53¾ seconds. Myers, however, was very unwell, and started against the advice of his friends to beat the record, which was then 52 1-5 sec. After running away from his field for the first three hundred yards he went to pieces, and was beaten in the last fifty yards. He soon redeemed himself however, and from that time to the present date has had things generally his own way in all scratch events, having only suffered defeat twice since in a run of that nature, and then his defeat can be attributed to over-confidence more than to lack of ability. No less than nine times has he broken fifty seconds for the quarter, and for the half he has done 1 min. 55 3-5 sec.; twice, 1 min. 56 sec.; twice, 1 min. 56⅛ sec., and many times has won in or about 2 minutes easily. In the spring of 1881 he sailed for England, and returned home in August of the same year after hav-

MARVIN'S "TONGUE & GROOVE" SAFE.

ing broken the English record at the quarter three separate times, and altered the English half-mile record from 1 min. 57½ sec. to 1 min. 56 sec., and doing it so easily that the best of English judges declared him able to do near 1 min. 50 sec. for this distance. His quarter mile record 48 3-5 sec. made at the English Championships in 1881, is not only the best Amateur, but the best record either Amateur or Professional, ever made on a properly surveyed track. Mr. Myers, up to 1882, won twenty-four championships, 15 of America, 8 of Canada, and one of England, and holds the following records:—

50 yards,	5½ seconds.					
100 "	10 "		500 yards,	58 seconds,		
120 "	12 "		600 "	1 m. 11 2-5 seconds,		
200 "	20⅛ "		660 "	1 m. 22 "		
220 "	22½ "		700 "	1 m. 31 "		
250 "	26 "		800 "	1 m. 44 2-5 "		
300 "	31 "		880 "	1 m. 55 2-5 "		
350 "	36 4-5 "		1000 "	2 m. 13 sec. American.		
400 "	43⅜ "		1000 "	2 m. 14 1-5 " English.		
440 "	48 3-5 " Eng.		1320 "	3 m. 13 "		
440 "	48¼ " Amer.		1 mile, 4 m. 27 3-5			

In 1880, at the Championship Meeting, he carried off the prizes for 100, 220, 440 and 880 yard runs, making extra fast time in every race (see records), while three days later he won the same four events at the Canadian Championship Meeting, thus winning 8 championships in one year—a feat never accomplished by any other athlete.

So it was in 1880 that L. E. Meyers began to do such fast running. He was now known to be the best runner in the country, and he began to break records right and left, not stopping at seemingly any figures. His athletic career has been distinguished by a series of victories and breaking of records, such as have not been credited to any athlete, either living or dead, for in the few years of his active athletic life he has broken every American record from 100 yards to one mile, has beaten all English and American athletes at his favorite distances, and has lowered the records for the ¼ mile, six hundred yards, one half-mile and one thousand yards runs to a point not attainable by any living athlete, either here or abroad, and to reach which, the athletes of years to come, will probably unsuccessfully struggle. His success has been truly phenomenal, while no athlete in the world has more friends nor true admirers than this young, world-renowned Champion runner. He has made three trips to Europe altogether, met the best and the fastest runners of our mother athletic country (England), and has not only beaten them all at favorite distances, but has also left them records far better than what they ever thought for. He has won over 300 prizes, consisting of medals, cups, watches, jewelry, canes, silver stands and athletic uniforms, and although he at first belonged to the Knickerbocker Yacht Club, with the exception of 4 or 5 races, he has carried the Manhattan colors through his many battles on the cinder path.

In 1880 at the Championship Meeting, Harry Fredricks won the one mile run in 4.39 3-5. J. S. Voorhees the broad jump, and L. H. Johnson the two mile bicycle race.

Mr. George H. Carr, President of the Club, has held this honorable position from the start, and too much credit cannot be given him for the successful manner in which he has conducted both the club and its athletes to fame and prosperity.

Among some of the most prominent athletes of this club may be mentioned the names of:—

L. E. Meyers,	T. J. Murphy,	Wm. McEwen,
Harry Pike,	S. Derickson,	Harry Fredricks,
A. G. Waldron,	L. P. Smith,	T. H. Smith,
J. S. Voorhees,	W. Storm,	C. S. Busse,
D. J. Tompkins,	F. S. Lambrecht,	C. L. Meyers,
W. C. White,	F. G. Abbott,	O. Bodelsen,
T. H. Burton,	W. McNichol,	R. A. Knight,
G. C. Walton,	L. A. Stuart,	W. T. Stoddard,
C. E. Schuyler,	H. M. Stone,	J. M. Young,
J. Magee,	A. J. Camacha,	J. B. White,
C. L. Jacquelin,	J. D. Freeman,	E. W. Brown,
Wm. H. Purdy,	W. O'Keefe,	A. T. Moore,
L. H. Johnson,	E. McCaffrey,	W. H. Griffin,
J. T. Graham,	E. D. Jesurun,	C. J. Cornell,
W. T. Bailey.		

The officers from year to year have been as follows:—

1877-'78.

PRESIDENT,
GEO. W. CARR.

VICE-PRESIDENT,   SECRETARY,   TREASURER,
W. C. FRANCE. JR.   GEO. D. PARMLY,   R. B. CULBERT.

CAPTAIN.
JOHN FRAZER.

FIRST LIEUTENANT,   SECOND LIEUTENANT,
W. H. GRIFFIN,   E. G. GURNEY.

TRUSTEES,
S. B. POMEROY,   HARRY P. PIKE,
GEO. W. THOMAS.

THE MANHATTAN ATHLETIC CLUB.

1879.

PRESIDENT,
GEO. W. CARR.

VICE-PRESIDENT,   TREASURER,   SECRETARY,
GEO. W. THOMAS.   WM. J. McEWEN.   R. B. CULBERT.

CAPTAIN,
HARRY P. PIKE.

FIRST LIEUTENANT,   SECOND LIEUTENANT,
W. H. GRIFFIN.   JAS. D. FREEMAN.

TRUSTEES,
S. B. POMEROY,   W. C. FRANCE, Jr.,
O. J. CONKLIN.

1880.

PRESIDENT.
GEO. W. CARR.

VICE-PRESIDENT,   SECRETARY,   TREASURER
GEO. W. THOMAS.   WM. J. McEWEN.   R. B. CULBERT.

CAPTAIN,
HARRY P. PIKE.

FIRST LIEUTENANT,   SECOND LIEUTENANT,
W. H. GRIFFIN.   H. BIRRELL.

TRUSTEES,
S. B. POMEROY,   W. C. FRANCE, Jr.,
GEO. C. BOWERS.

1881.

PRESIDENT,
GEO. W. CARR.

VICE-PRESIDENT,   SECRETARY,   TREASURER,
GEO. W. THOMAS.   W. NEWBROUGH.   S. B. POMEROY.

CAPTAIN,
HARRY P. PIKE.

FIRST LIEUTENANT,   SECOND LIEUTENANT,
T. A. McEWEN.   J. D. FREEMAN.

TRUSTEES,
G. A. AVERY,   GEO. C. BOWERS,
J. MAGEE.

THE MANHATTAN ATHLETIC CLUB.

1882.

PRESIDENT,
GEO. W. CARR.

VICE-PRESIDENT, SECRETARY, TREASURER,
G. W. THOMAS. F. J. GRAHAM. S. B. POMEROY.

CAPTAIN,
C. J. CONNELL.

FIRST LIEUTENANT, SECOND LIEUTENANT,
G. M. L. SACKS. W. H. PURDY.

TRUSTEES,
G. A. AVERY, C. E. TROTTER,
JAS. MAGEE.

1883.

PRESIDENT,
GEO. W. CARR.

VICE-PRESIDENT, SECRETARY, TREASURER,
GEO. W. THOMAS. L. E. MYERS. G. M. L. SACKS.

CAPTAIN,
CHAS. J. CONNELL.

FIRST LIEUTENANT, SECOND LIEUTENANT,
P. ST. G. BISSELL. WALTON STORM.

TRUSTEES,
GEO. A. AVERY, H. W. BERLIN,
CHAS. E. TROTTER.

1884.

PRESIDENT,
GEO. W. CARR.

VICE-PRESIDENT, SECRETARY, TREASURER,
CHAS. E. TROTTER. L. E. MYERS. WALTON STORM.

CAPTAIN,
SAMUEL J. CORNELL.

FIRST LIEUTENANT, SECOND LIEUTENANT,
GEO. F. KNUBEL. WM. R. BEERS.

TRUSTEES,
GEO. A. AVERY, JAMES MAGEE,
CHAS. W. MINOR.

THE MANHATTAN ATHLETIC CLUB.

1885.

PRESIDENT,
GEO. W. CARR.

VICE-PRESIDENT,	TREASURER,	SECRETARY,
C. E. TROTTER.	L. P. SMITH.	WALTON STORM.

CAPTAIN,
L. A. STUART.

FIRST LIEUTENANT,		SECOND LIEUTENANT,
J. W. MAGEE.		S. S. SCHUYLER.

TRUSTEES,

GEO. A. AVERY,		E. S. APPLEBY,
	C. C. HUGHS.	

Harry Frdericks, the amateur champion mile runner of America or several years, is 22 years old, 5 feet 4 inches in height, and weighs 123 lbs. For the past five years he has won the mile race at the championship meeting, never having been pushed. His best record is 4 minutes 32 3-5 seconds; but what he could do if he were compelled to run out is unknown. His friends only know that in practice for special races he has beaten the best American record.

Arthur Waldron, the amateur champion one hundred yard runner of America, is 22 years old, 5 feet 7 inches in height, and weighs 118 lbs. For two years he won the 100 yards race at the champion meeting. His race at the meeting in 1883, when he beat Brooks, showed him to be the equal, if not the superior, of any sprinter in America. With heavy odds in Brooks' favor, Waldron won in 10¼ seconds. Of this race, the *Spirit of the Times* saying: "The wind blew freshly in the faces of "the runners, and the performance was really as meritorious as several of our 10 second records."

This club may well be called the finest athletic organization in America, for surely the Manhattan colors are seen at every meeting of any importance, and the many young champion athletes are always striving for their club's success on the cinder path, whether at home or abroad, and they seldom leave for home without taking with them a good share of the prizes.

The club colors are white and with a red diamond lapping at the ends.

The proposed gymnasium mentioned in connection with this club has now taken the form of a club house, and an agreement has been made with the Manhattan Club Building Association, a company incorporated by Mr. Wm. J. Swan, to lease for a term of 21 years a spacious and commodious club-house which is to be erected on the corner of Madison Avenue and 59th Street. Work on the structure will be commenced at once and pushed with all possible haste to completion. The edifice will be an imposing one, and is to cost over $200,000. When furnished it will be the best equipped athletic establishment in the world.

This club house will be three full stories in height, with an elevation of 70 feet, and will be built of brick and terra cotta, the plans and specifications being already perfected.

The basement floor will contain a magnificent bowling room, with eight full sized alleys. Adjoining this will be the swimming bath, the dimensions of which will be 70x20 (with a spring board plunge of 15 feet), the Russian baths, and dressing and lounging rooms. The cafe and barber shop will also be on this floor.

The entrance to the club-house will be on the corner of Madison avenue and Fifty-ninth street, and on entering, after passing the club offices and coat room, one comes to the parlor, a magnificent room fifty feet square, divided in the centre by columns. The parlor faces on Madison avenue, and the windows are but five feet above the sidewalk. The rest of the floor is occupied by the restaurant, 25x75, the library, smoking room, and directors' room.

On the second floor will be a beautiful concert room, with stage, and all modern conveniences for private theatricals. The floor will be finished so that it can be used for dancing and also for tennis, and ample space has been set apart for dressing rooms, etc. The billiard room will be 25x70, and will contain six billiard and two pool tables.

The third floor will be occupied entirely by the gymnasium, the floor of which will be 60x90 in the clear. The ceiling will be twenty-one feet high, with a sliding skylight 20x50; this will give perfect light and ventilation at all times. On the gymnasium floor will also be the dressing rooms and lockers, and also a plunge and a vapor bath, with toilets, etc. Twelve feet above the gymnasium floor will be the running track. This, instead of being the ordinary gymnasium track, will be a cinder track, so that athletes may enjoy all the benefits of out-door training. The track will be eighteen laps to the mile.

On the level with the track will be dressing rooms, lockers, a padded boxing room, 25x25, a fencing room, shower baths, toilets, etc. An Otis elevator will run from the basement to the running track floor. The building will be as near fire-proof as possible; the staircases, of which there will be three, being absolutely fire-proof. The building will be lighted by electricity and also by gas.

The charge for billiards, bowling, etc., will be nominal; less than half the usual cost.

The club will retain its athletic track at Eighty-sixth street and Eighth avenue, which will be improved so as to favorably compete with any athletic grounds in the world, and it is the intention of the club to procure a plot of land on the Harlem river, and erect thereon a boat house, which will be equipped in the most perfect manner.

The club house is to be completed October 1, 1886.

THE BENEFITS OF ROWING.

Rowing is admitted by all authorities to be the most beneficial of exercises, because it calls into play every muscle in the body and gives to each one a full and equal share of work. Five minutes of brisk rowing will produce a rapid circulation of the blood, free perspiration, cause the lungs at each inspiration to fill themselves to their full capacity, and thus enlarge the chest and vitalize the blood, without unduly straining any of the muscles. This condition of the body cannot be obtained from any other form of exercise in the same time without making one set of muscles do all the work, and so seriously laming them.

Rowing, therefore, is an excellent substitute for the gymnasium.

If ladies would devote a small portion of each day to this exercise, they would soon secure that freshness of complexion and roundness of limb, so indicative of perfect digestion and circulation; and "nervousness" would be unknown, except as a memory of the past.

I am now enabled to offer to my patrons and customers "A Perfect Parlor Rowing Apparatus." After spending thousands of dollars, and years in experiments, with the combined help of the best mechanical engineering talent, I have produced a perfect and simple device which will not break or get out of order, as has been the trouble in my former and all other apparatuses. In my improved machine there are no springs, as the pressure is regulated exclusively by friction and can be varied by an adjusting thumbscrew by the will of the operator. The clutching or gripping device is simple and positive in its movements, to which the oar is attached, and allows the operators to rest their hands upon the oars and feathering same when coming back, in the same manner as ordinary rowing. As each oar is provided with an independent friction the operator can let either oar rest and apply both hands to one oar and pick up the other at any time again. And I have so arranged the machine, that by changing the outrigger and oars about on the frame, the pushing of the oars may be practiced similar to the style of the Norwegian sailor, which is the best exercise for developing the muscles of the back and stomach. To insure the confidence I have in my machine, I will warrant it.

Each machine is provided with a counter or indicator, which is so graduated that one revolution of the dial is equivalent to one quarter of a mile as calculated from Hanlon's time at the thirty-two strokes per minute, which will be found of great benefit in regulating the time spent in this exercise, especially in boating clubs, training schools and gymnasiums, where racing can be done at seasons when it cannot be tried on the water.

Send stamp for book on Physical Culture to

J. M. LAFLIN,
200 Broadway, New York.

Price $10.00.

HINTS ON EXERCISING.

Every year, for the past ten or twenty years, athletics have taken a strong hold on the minds of all the young and many of the old of both sexes. The first athletic clubs were made up of young men who, for the most part, excelled in some exercise or other, or of those who, being confined most of the time by business cares, wished merely for a little relaxation.

These clubs could not, of course, afford elegant or costly clubhouses for members who only joined them to display their athletic accomplishments or to be able to spend a few of their leisure evenings in a sort of semi-barbarous condition in the freedom of a free-and-easy gymnasium. As the interest in physical training and muscular development became more general, and ladies began to encourage the amateur meetings by their presence, the niceties soon came to be more closely looked after, and the houses and grounds of the clubs which made a specialty of athletics were improved, till at the present time the palatial homes of some of the principal athletic clubs in this country and in England are second to none in the luxury and elegance of their appointments.

There are now thousands of young men in this city alone who, too much lacking in confidence in their own powers, are, instead of joining one of the athletic clubs, by spasmodic and often ill-judged attempts at exercising at home, doing themselves more harm than good. It is to this class far more than to any other that a writer on athletics should endeavor to reach.

Young men belonging to athletic clubs have little need of being urged to properly exercise themselves. As quickly as their feet touch the track of the club they have just joined, the eyes of the trackmaster and half the members of the club are bent upon them, to try and discover any symptom of their being embryo amateur champions; and if such signs are seen, all possible efforts are used to induce the stranger to develop himself in the particular direction he seems inclined to, with the hope that in time the club may shine with reflected honor from his well-won glory.

It is to the young men whose inability, either through tightness of purse or lack of time, cannot join the clubs, that instruction should be given. In the first place, a very moderate amount of exercise of the proper kind, and taken at suitable times, will in a very reasonable period produce a good appetite, a better digestion, sound sleep, greater strength, first-class health, and a much clearer and stronger business mind, with more moral perceptions. This statement does not now need proof, although it took a many years' battle to establish it as thoroughly as it now is in most minds. All that is asked of any unbeliever is a fair trial.

It is not necessary for one who desires to reap the advantage of physical training to go to the expense and trouble that some lovers of exercise do. The poorest person, even if his livelihood is gained entirely by a sedentary occupation, can, if he knows how, by ten minutes' work alone in his sleeping-room every night and morning, gain a great deal more than could possibly be expected. If one can afford it, a few fixtures which will not cost much had better be purchased. A rowing-machine and punching-bag are the best and least expensive contrivances, and the things with which the most can be done. They will cost less than twenty dollars set up ready to handle; they can be bought of any of the big athletic goods houses (see Laflin's advertisement), and the list might be greatly extended. The rowing-machine is a gymnasium in itself, if a good one, and what exercise the rowing-machine does not permit he may get without fail from the punching-bag and the bar from which it hangs.

The best or most convenient seasons for exercise will be, for most people, on rising and retiring. The exercising should be done with the athlete in as little clothing as possible, in order to give perfect freedom for all the movements and a good chance for a sort of air-bath, which most people find very beneficial. The movements should be quick and decided, but heavy weights should be most decidedly barred. More persons have been injured by lifting heavy weights than have ever been benefitted by them. Ten or fifteen minutes' exercise with light weights, the rowing-machine and the punching-bag, will cause the perspiration to pour from all parts of the body in almost any sort of weather. As soon as the exercise is ended, a bath-towel should be used to wipe dry; then a cold plunge, shower or sponge-bath should be indulged in. This is very important, especially in the summer time, and should never be neglected. In warm weather the body should only be wiped dry—not rubbed dry, as in cold weather, as rubbing promotes the circulation and causes a sensation of warmth. The exercise should be rapid and vigorous, but not sufficiently so as to compel one to stop because of lack of breath. The exercise should be kept up always for a little time after the muscles fairly ache. The muscles ache because of the blood being forced into them to enable them to meet the demands being made upon them. This excess of blood causes them to swell and make them ache. It is a law of nature always to try to make up for deficiencies, and if constant calls are made upon the muscles to do more work than they have been accustomed to perform, they soon swell and increase in size and strength to accomplish what is asked of them. Physiology teaches that a muscle which has been thus swelled by exercise returns to its natural state in about three days. This is also known because one is always more or less lame for about three days after some unusual muscular feat. It is easily seen, therefore, that to develop the muscles markedly, one must exercise enough to get them quite tired at least once in three days.

TABLE

Showing the Digestibility of the Most Common Articles of Food.

Food	Preparation	Hour.Min.
Beef	Roasted	3.00
Beefsteak	Broiled	3.00
"	Fried	4.00
Corned Beef	Boiled	4.15
Mutton	Roasted	3.15
Lamb	Boiled	2.30
Pork	Roasted	5.15
"	Fried	4.15
Sausage	Fried	4.00
Sucking Pig	Roasted	2.30
Pigs' Feet	Soused	1.00
Veal	Boiled	4.00
Venison Steak	Broiled	1.35
Chicken	Fricaseed	3.45
Fowls	Roasted	4.00
Ducks	Roasted	4.00
Turkey	Roasted	2.30
Eggs	Hard Boiled	3.30
"	Soft Boiled	3.00
Oysters	Raw	2.55
"	Stewed	3.30
Milk		2.15
Trout or Salmon	Boiled	1.45
Tripe	Fried	1.30
Striped Bass	Boiled	3.00
Soup, Barley		1.30
" Beef and Vegetables		4.00
" Chicken		3.00
Potatoes	Boiled	3.30
String Beans	Boiled	2.30
Succotash	Boiled	3.45
Beets	Boiled	3.45
Cabbage	Boiled	4.30
Carrots	Boiled	3.15
Parsnips	Boiled	2.30
Rice	Boiled	1.00
Turnips	Boiled	3.30
Wheat Bread		3.30
Corn "		3.15
Cheese	Old	3.30
Apple Dumplings	Boiled	3.00
Oatmeal		3.30

AMATEUR OARSMAN DEFINITIONS.

AN AMATEUR

As defined by the National Association of Amateur Oarsmen.

We define an amateur to be—"One who does not enter in an open competition; or for either a stake, public or admission money, or entrance fee ; or compete with or against a professional for any prize ; who has never taught, pursued, or assisted in the pursuit o athletic exercises as a means of livelihood ; whose membership of any rowing or other athletic club was not brought about, or does not continue, because of any mutual agreement or understanding, expressed or implied, whereby his becoming or continuing a member of such club would be of any pecuniary benefit to him whatever, direct or indirect, and who has never been employed in any occupation involving any use of oar or paddle ;" (as adopted August 18, 1872, and amended January 20, 1876) and who shall otherwise conform to the rules and regulations of the National Association of Amateur Oarsman.

Definitions taking effect April 26, 1884:

A Junior Sculler

Is one who has never pulled in a Senior race, or won a Junior "Scull race."

A Junior Oarsman

"Is one who has not pulled an oar in a Senior race, or been a winning oarsman in a Junior race."

Competitions with members of his own club will not affect the standing, as a junior, of any oarsman or sculler.

The qualifications of a Junior Oarsman or Sculler shall relate to each time of his coming to the starting post, whether in a trial or a final heat.

PROGRAMME FOR CHAMPIONSHIP REGATTA.

Senior Single Sculls,	Pair-oared Shells,
Junior " "	8-oared Shells,
Senior Four-oared Shells,	Junior Four-oared Shells.
Double Sculls.	

AMATEUR CHAMPION OARSMEN OF AMERICA.

WINNERS OF PREVIOUS REGATTAS.

EIGHT OARED SHELLS. *Time.*

1880—At Philadelphia, Pa., July 9, Dauntless R. C......8 m 55 s.
1881—At Washington, D. C., September 9, Narragansett B. C.................................7 m. 51¼ s.
1883—At Newark, N. J., August 8, Metropolitan R. C....7 m. 51 s.
1884—At Watkins, N. J., August 13, Columbia B. C. W. O..8 m. 22 s.
1885—At Boston, Mass., August 13, Columbia B. C....7 m. 46¾ s.

JUNIOR FOUR-OARED SHELLS. *Time.*

1882—At Detroit, Mich., August 9, Detroit B. C.......10 m. 22 s.
1883—At Newark, N. J., August 8, Alcoyne B. C......8 m. 16¼ s.
1884—At Watkins, N. Y., August 13, Watkins R. A....9 m. 1½ s.
1885—At Boston, Mass., August 13, Dirigo B. C........8 m. 31 s.

DOUBLE SCULLS. *Time.*

1873—At Philadelphia, Pa., October 8, Steele & Witmar: Crescent B. C................................9 m. 30 s.
1874—At Troy, N. Y., September 4, Yates & Curtis: N. Y. Athletic Club..............................9 m. 37¼ s.
1875—At Troy, N. Y., September 1, Robinson & Courtney: Union Springs B. C.........................8 m. 50½ s.
1876—At Philadelphia, Pa., August 23, Robinson & Courtney: Union Springs B. C....................9 m. 19 s.
1877—At Detroit, Mich., August 15, McBeath & Henderson: Quaker City B. C....................8 m. 18 s.
1878—At Newark, N. J., August 21, O'Donnell & Powers: Hope R. C .... 8 m. 37¼ s.
1879—At Saratoga, N. Y., July 10, Rathborne & Lyon: N Y. Athletic Club....... .. .. 9 m. 18¾ s.
1880—At Philadelphia, Pa., July 9, Whitaker & Holmes: Pawtucket B. C ....9 m. 41 s.
1881—At Washington, D. C., September 9, Appley & Holmes: Pawtucket B. C ....8 m. 37½ s.
1882—At Detroit, Mich., August 9, O'Connell & Buckley; Portland B. C................... .... 9 m. 30 s.
1883—At Newark, N. J., August 8, O'Connell & Buckley: Portland, B. C. .. ..·········......8 m. 16 s.
1884—At Watkins, N. Y., August 13, Toronto B. C .....9 m. 10 s.
1885—At Boston, Mass., August 13th, M. F. & T. H. Monahan: Albany R. C................ .....9 m. 4½ s.

SENIOR FOUR-OARED SHELLS. Time.

1873—At Philadelphia, Pa., October 8, Argonauta R. A.. 8 m. 16 s.
1874—At Troy, N. Y., September 4, Beaverwyck R, C..8 m. 45½ s.
1875—At Troy, N. Y., September 1, Atalanta B. C.....8 m. 34¼ s.
1876—At Philadelphia, Pa., August 24, Atalanta B. C...9 m. 36¾ s
1877—At Detroit, Mich., August 15, Emerald B. C......7 m. 50 s.
1878—At Newark, N. J., August 21, Mutuel B. C.........8 m. 4 s.
1879—At Saratoga, N. Y., July 11, Hillsdale R. C.....8 m. 32¾ s.
1880—At Philadelphia, Pa., July 9, Hillsdale R. C......8 m. 53 s.
1881—At Washington D. C., September 9, Hillsdale R. C. 8 m. 6½ s.
1882—At Detroit, Mich., August 9, Centennial B C......8 m. 27 s.
1883—At Newark, N. J., August 8, Eureka B. C......8 m. 16¼ s.
1884—At Watkins, N. Y., August 13th, Argonaut B. C.. 8 m. 22¾ s.
1885—At Boston, Mass., August 13th, Nautilus R. C. . 8 m. 23 s.

SENIOR SINGLE SCULLS. Time.

1873—At Philadelphia, Pa., October 8, Chas Myers: Nassau B. C...................................10 m. 8¼ s.
1874—At Troy, N. Y., September 4, F. E. Yates: N. Y. Athletic Club.........................10 m. 16½ s.
1875—At Troy, N. Y., September 1, Charles E. Courtney: Union Springs B. C............................9 m. 46 s.
1876—At Philadelphia, Pa., August 24, F. E. Yates: Union Springs B. C....................... .... 10 m. 39½ s.
1877—At Detroit, Mich., August 16, George W. Lee: Triton B. C.........................'.........................9 m. 11 s.
1878—At Newark, N. J., August 21, George W. Lee, Triton B. C...............................9 m. ¾ s.
1879—At Saratoga, N. Y., July 11, F. J. Mumford: Hope R. C..9 m. 50 s.
1880—At Philadelphia, Pa., July 9, F. J. Mumford: Perseverance B. C........................;........10 m. 5¾ s.
1881—At Washington, D. C., September 9, F. E. Holmes: Pawtucket B. C............................9 m. 6¾ s.
1882—At Detroit, Mich., August 9, F. E. Holmes: Pawtucket B. C..................... ....10 m. 5 s.
1883—At Newark, N. J., August 8, Joseph Laing: Grand Trunk B. C.............................. 8 m. 44 s.
1884—At Watkins, N. Y., August 13, Joseph Laing: Grand Trunk B. C.............................9 m. 28¼ s.
1885—At Boston, Mass., August 13,. E. J. Murphy......9 m. 42 s.

AMATEUR CHAMPION OARSMEN. 91

JUNIOR SINGLE SCULLS. *Time.*

1878—At Newark, N. J., August 21, George Bowlsby, Jr.,
Amateur B. C................................. 9 m. 40 s.
1879—At Saratoga, N. Y., July 11, W. Murray, Elizabeth
B. C.. 10 m. 1½ s.
1880—At Philadelphia. Pa., July 9, J. A. Whitaker, Pawtucket B. C................................. 10 m. 43¾ s.
1881—At Washington, D. C., September 9, A. T. O'Brien,
Dolphin B. C................................ 9 m. 42½ s.
1882—At Detroit, Mich., August 9, John J. Murphy,
Shawmut B. C................................ 9 m. 48 s.
1883—At Newark, N. J., August 8, J. Kilion, Bradford
B. C.. 9 m. 20½ s.
1884—At Watkins, N. Y., August 13th, E. J. Mulcahy,
Albany B. C................................. 10 m. 1 s.
1885—At Boston, Mass., August 13th, Peter Snyder,
Columbia B. C............................... 9 m. 34 s.

PAIR OARED SHELLS. *Time.*

1874—At Troy, N. Y., September 4, Smith & Eldred,
Argonauta R. A.............................. 9 w. 41½ s.
1875—At Troy, N. Y., August 31, Smith & Eldred: Argonauta R. A................................... 9 m. 39 s.
1876—At Philadelphia, Pa., August 23, Downs & Eustis:
Atalanta B. C............................... 10 m. 10¾ s.
1877—At Detroit, Mich., August 16, Smith & Kiloran:
Emerald B. C................................ 9 m. 4 s.
1878—At Newark, N. J., August 20, Bulger & Graves: Mutuel B. C................................... 8 m. 56¾ s.
1879—At Saratoga, N. Y., July 9, Gorman Bros.: Olympic B. C.................................... 9 m. 41¾ s.
1880—At Philadelphia, Pa., July 9, Gorman Bros.: Albany
R. C.. 10 m. 7½ s.
1881—At Washington, D. C., September 9, Clegg & Stand-
ish: Detroit Scullers........................ 6 m. 33 s.
1882—At Detroit, Mich. August 9, Bulger & Moseley:
Mutual B. C................................. 10 m. 38 s.
1883—At Newark, N. J., August 8, Bulger & Moseley, Mutual B. C................................... 8 m. 54 s.
1884—At Watkins, N. Y., August 13, Moseley & Bulger:
Albany B. C................................. W. O.
1885—At Boston, Mass., August 13, Fred Freeman and
John Weldon: Ariel B. C..................... 9 m. 33 s.

The Kill Von Kull Rowing Association.

This Association, which is now one of the best known organizations of oarsmen in the country, was organized in 1880. It comprises the following strong boat clubs, viz:

The Argonauta Rowing Association, Bayonne Rowing Association, and Viking Rowing Association, of Bayonne City. The Staten Island Athletic Club and Clifton Boat Club, of Staten Island. The Alcyone Rowing Association, and Arthur-Kull Rowing Association, of Elizabeth.

At the first three annual Regattas all these clubs, but the Clifton, were represented, and in the last two regattas every club in the Association contested one or more of the races.

These regattas have always excited great interest among oarsmen, and the official record of the time made has invariably been accepted without question in boating circles throughout the country, a fact which speaks volumes as to the standing and management of the Association.

The regattas have usually been held upon the Kills, but as this course is objectionable for many reasons, it was decided at the annual meeting of the Association, held May 9, to hold the regatta this year on the Newark Bay course. In referring to this action of the Association, the *Bayonne Times* says:—

"A new course was selected which will meet with the approval of all oarsmen in this city as well as the majority from adjoining sections. It is on Newark Bay, commencing one mile east of the club house of the Newark Bay Boat Club and ending at the club house. This Club has tendered the use of their pretty house for the occasion, and the regatta was one of the principal boating events of the season. Oarsmen as a rule acknowledge this course to be the most desirable, all things considered, that is to be found in the vicinity of New York."

The officers of the Kill Von Kull Association for this year are as follows:—

William C. Davis, of the Staten Island Athletic Club, President.
Pierson Haviland, of the Argonauta Rowing Association, Secretary and Treasurer.

REGATTA COMMITTEE.

R. C. Annett, of the Argonautas.
W. A. Lentilhon, of the Staten Island Athletic Club.
Joseph Elsworth, of the Bayonnes.
George A. Squire, of the Newark Bay Boat Club.

The Argonauta Rowing Association,
BERGEN POINT.

This Association was organized April 5, 1870, and incorporated.

At first the Argonauta Club was purely a social organization, but as the members became proficient in the use of the oar, they became ambitious to try conclusions with their more athletic neighbors. After being defeated twice by the Neptune Boat Club, of Staten Island, and once by the Vesper Club, of Yonkers, a crew composed of Messrs. Schuyler, Craft, Stephenson, Phillips, Humphreys and Bramhall, met the Oneidas, of Jersey City, and gracefully took them into camp.

In 1872 the Club sent to the front a crew composed of Smith, Bramhall, Stephenson and Eldred, which afterward achieved a national reputation. This crew met the Neptunes in the third contest between the two clubs, and wrested the "Whip of the Kills" from the unwilling hands of the Staten Island Club in the extraordinary short time of 15 m. 5¼ s. for three miles.

Then commenced a series of victories in the home waters, and at Philadelphia, Harlem and elsewhere, which placed the name of "Argonauta" among the most famous of amateur clubs; Walter Man, after the first season, occupying No. 2 seat, vice E. J. Bramhall, retired.

From the date of its organization up to the present time, the Club has competed in forty-nine races with other clubs in match races and regattas (not including trial heats), and has won thirty of these races, rowing in many instances against the fastest and most formidable crews in the country.

Twenty-seven sets of colors and banners, trophies of victory adorn the walls of the club parlor, besides photographs of the National, Interlaken and other challenge cups won in important regattas.

The Club won the Championship of the United States three times in four-oared shells, four times in pair-oared shells, held the Schuylkill Navy Championship three successive years, the Greenwood Lake Championship two years, and has retained the "Whip of the Kills" from 1872 to this day.

Notwithstanding the intense interest in the racing competition with other clubs, care was taken to keep up the social character of the organization, and maintain its high standing in the community. Indeed the Argonautas are noted for the cordial manner in which the hospitalities of the Club are always extended to visitors.

The Club House is beautifully situated upon a lot 183 by 75 feet, owned by the Association, and is splendidly arranged and handsomely furnished.

The club is in excellent financial condition, and we hope it will enjoy many years of prosperity.

The present roll of active members includes representatives of most of the best known families on the Point, and the honorary list comprises many old and prominent citizens who worthily served as active members in former years.

The officers are as follows:—

E. W. Humphreys, President.
E. R. Craft, First Vice-President.
N. W. Trask, Second Vice President.
H. A. Craft, Treasurer.
M. V. Stringham, Recording Secretary.
J. W. Goddard, Corresponding Secretary.
Pierson Haviland, Captain.
R. C. Annett, Lieutenant.

The Viking Rowing Association.
BAYONNE.

Organized 1873. This association was organized by the union of the Elizabeth Boat Club and the Triton Boat Club, of Pamrapo, N. J.

The combined membership of these two clubs numbered about twenty, and the new organization started with about this number. In the spring of 1877 a new boat house was built opposite the depot at Bayonne, N. J., which has since been kept in excellent condition, and is now fully equipped to meet the requirements of the members. Since the organization of the club its membership has been largely increased, until now it has fully 50 members, or more than double the number on the roll in 1875.

The Club is very prosperous and is on a sound financial basis, with no debt on the house or other property. Its fleet of boats comprise four-oared shells, pair-oared gigs, and barges, all comparatively new boats and in good shape. In addition to the annual club Regattas and races for challenge cups and badges, the Vikings have competed in many Regattas at Newark, Rutherford, Greenwood Lake, Harlem, and on the Kill Von Kull, and in several match races, notably with the Bayonnes and Arthur-Kulls.

The Viking Rowing Association is entitled to the enviable distinction of being the pioneer Club in the movement which resulted in the organization of the Kill Von Kull Rowing Association.

The officers at present are as follows:—

S. D. Housten, President.
James L. Meyers, Vice-President.
T. C. Hanna, Secretary.
W. B. Seaman, Treasurer.
H. E. Duncan, Jr., Captain.
W. P. Thomas, Lieutenant.

The Bayonne Rowing Association.
BAYONNE.

Organized 1872, incorporated 1875. This well-known association of oarsmen was started principally for the purpose of having a Club House which could be used by the young men in Bayonne who were interested in boating. A one-story building was erected on the New York Bay shore opposite the depot, and this for a while answered the purpose.

Shortly after the organization of the Club a six-oared gig and a four-oared barge were procured. The entire membership of the Club at that time was not enough to man both boats at once. These boats were heavy pleasure boats, and, in fact, were of the class commonly known among oarsmen as "beef boats," so that the Club was hardly fitted to engage in either challenge races or regattas. Nevertheless when, in 1874, the Oneida Boat Club of Jersey City (now the Hudson) challenged The Bayonne Rowing Association to a three-mile six-oared gig race, the boys pluckily determined to make up a crew and row the race in their heavy gig.

This race excited great interest in Bayonne, and was hotly contested from start to finish, the Oneidas being declared winners by half a length by the referee, against the protest of the Bayonne representatives.

The great interest taken in the race, and the grit and determination shown by the Bayonne crew (who had no practical training) in rowing against a thoroughly trained picked crew from one of the strongest boat clubs in existence, at that time, resulted in a popular subscription being taken up in Bayonne to assist the Club in building a suitable club house, and to purchase such boats as were necessary for racing purposes.

Twelve hundred dollars were raised by this subscription and turned over to the Club. In the fall of the same year building operations were commenced, and rapidly pushed until the present handsome boat house was finished. The total cost of this building was $5,000, of which $1,200 was paid in cash, and the balance, $3,800, provided for by bond and mortgage. Almost as soon as building operations were commenced new members began to come into the Club, and in 1875, when it was incorporated, the Club roster contained the names of over forty members, among whom were many of the best known residents.

In order to liquidate the indebtedness on the club-house a sinking fund was established whereby one-sixth of the entire income was reserved to be applied solely to the reduction of the debt, which by this means was decreased every year, until in 1882 the total indebtedness was only $2,800.

In the early part of 1883 it became necessary to make some arrangements to pay off a portion of the mortgage. After careful consideration of the matter it was decided to hold a fair, which was done in June, 1883, and in June of the following year the experiment was repeated. The two fairs resulted in a net profit to the club of $3,900.

This splendid success was largely due to the untiring efforts of President W. H. Jasper, and the excellent management and harmonious action of the ladies and gentlemen who composed the Fair Committees.

The money raised in this way cleared the club of debt, enabled it to invest about $1,000 in much-needed boats with which to send out crews properly equipped, and to put the club-house in excellent condition.

For several years the Bayonne Rowing Association has given a series of bi-weekly sociables at their club-house, which have been attended by the *elite* of Bayonne City, and which are very popular.

Since its organization the Bayonne Rowing Association has participated in many regattas and challenge races, in addition to the annual club regatta, and many handsome trophies adorn the club-house.

The following are among its most notable victories :—

    Pair-oared shell, at Rutherford Park, 1875;
    Four-oared barge, Kills Regatta, 1881;
    "   "   "   1882;
    "   "   "   1883;
    Pair-oared gig,   "   1884;
    Four-oared barge,   "   1885;

and four-oared shell, three miles, in 1873, which was a challenge match race with the Vikings for the Championship.

The Bayonne Rowing Association is now in splendid shape, does not owe a dollar, and is well provided with first-class boats and the material to "whoop 'em up."

The following comprise the officers :—

    E. H. Bennett, President.
    Jos. Elsworth, Jr., Vice-President.
    Geo. E. Squire, Treasurer.
    J. A. Phillips, Jr., Secretary.
    E. E. Van Buskirk, Captain.
    C. O. Stillman, Lieutenant.

BOARD OF TRUSTEES :

    E. H. Bennett, Chairman.

Geo. A. Squire,	I. A. Gard,
E. E. Van Buskirk,	W. C. Nicholson,
Ernest C. Webb,	W. H. Jasper,
J. T. Field,	J. H. Allaire.

The Newark Bay Boat Club.
BAYONNE.

Organized May, 1881, incorporated October 3, 1882. In the Spring of 1881, some of the residents of Bay View Place, popularly called the Nine Row, after grumbling at each other about the lack of boating facilities on the beautiful shore of Newark Bay, and the need of a proper landing for boats and their freight of pleasure-seeking parties, finally concluded that something must be done or life would be a burden. What they attempted to do and how well they succeeded, it is the purpose of this sketch to tell.

On a beautiful May day, in the year 1881, six young men with ambitious longings, clustered together under the friendly branches of a "spreading chestnut tree," on what is now part of the club grounds, and held a long and secret pow-wow about some momentous question.

What were they, Nihilists or dynamiters, plotting some fearful and sanguinary crime to startle the world? No, gentle reader, they were the advanced guard, the "BIG SIX" who decided on that eventful May day to charge the nearest lumber yard and sieze in exchange for the paper promises of Uncle Sam, the material necessary to erect, not a fort, but a peaceful structure which would answer the purposes of a landing place for boats, and a resting place where the moonlight nights might be comfortably enjoyed literally on the Bay.

These young men were Messrs. George G. Jewett, Ernest C. Webb, Henry Garretson, William G. Goebel, Joseph A. Phillips, Jr., and E. Y. Phillips. and they immediately organized the Newark Bay Boat Club, becoming its charter members; a distinction none of them would exchange for the highest office in the gift of the Club.

Once started, the work was rapidly advanced, and in the following June a long dock or pier with landing steps and a covered platform with seating accommodations at the end, was completed, and this, with some additions, comprised for two seasons the Club House of the Newark Bay Boat Club.

The Club soon became very popular in Bayonne, and its dock a place of resort for ladies and gentlemen, who found there, and as they do now at the Club House, that cordial welcome which has made a visit to the Newark Bay Boat Club a pleasure to all who have enjoyed its hospitalities, and a matter of pride to our residents who take their visiting friends to see the Club House, as one of the attractions of summer life in Bayonne.

The popularity of the Club increased. Its membership grew so rapidly that in the summer of 1882, a Club House of some kind became not only the wish of all, but an absolute necessity in order to accommodate the members, their families and friends.

The idea of a club house having once taken root soon became the all-important question for consideration, and in the fall of 1882,

THE NEWARK BAY BOAT CLUB.

the club decided to issue five dollar bonds to the requisite amount in order to raise the necessary funds. This was done, and the money raised during the following winter—the bonds being placed at five per cent. interest.

In the following spring the building operations were commenced, and in June, 1883, the Club House was practically finished, and on July 2, 1883, the opening reception was held, and was attended by over 700 invited guests.

The Club House is beautifully situated on leased grounds at the west end of Bayonne avenue, and has a frontage on Newark Bay of sixty-five feet; is forty-five feet deep, with a ten-foot piazza, extending entirely around the second story. It has a deck roof. It was built under the personal supervision of the late Mr. Jacob C. Garretson, the architect, and we think that, for club purposes, it eclipses any building of its kind in the State.

The total cost of erecting the Club House was $3,500, and the present indebtedness is $2,300, the Club having paid $1,200 up to January last, or in a year and a half.

This is a record of which the members are justly proud, and, in appealing to their friends for the first time (through the medium of a Fair) they met with a liberal and generous response from the citizens of the City of Bayonne.

One distinctive feature of the Club since its organization has been its social character. The greatest care has been taken to make the Club House a pleasant place for ladies, and one where they can feel perfectly at home, and in which they can take the same interest as though they were in fact members. To this alone the success of the Club is due in a great measure.

It is admitted by all that the Club has been a benefit to Bayonne. It has been the means of attracting many families to the city who have become permanent residents, and it has provided a place for innocent amusement and recreation, which has been of great value to young men.

The following comprise the officers for this year:—

Ernest C. Webb, President.
John C. Bouton, Vice-President.
E. W. Snyder, Treasurer.
L. W. Amerman, Recording Secretary.
Arthur C. Webb, Corresponding Secretary.
Eugene McDonald, Captain.
Harry G. Stephens, Lieutenant.

TRUSTEES,

George A. Squire, Chairman.   L. W. Amerman, Secretary.
Ernest C. Webb.   George G. Jewett.
Sterling F. Hayward.   John C. Carragan.
Frank G. Bennett.   John A. Serrell.
DeWitt Van Buskirk.

Staten Island Rowing Club,

NEW BRIGHTON, S. I.

The Staten Island Rowing Club was established at New Brighton, Staten Island, in the spring of 1878, with a membership of fifty and the following officers : —

    A. P. Stokes, President.
    H. L. Horton, Vice-President.
    E. Kelly, Captain.
    G. B. West, Secretary.
    G. S. McCulloh, Treasurer.
    C. D. Ingersoll, Lieutenant.

TRUSTEES :

A. P. Stokes,	G. B. West,
H. R. Kelly,	H. L. Horton,
G. S. McCulloh,	Beverley Duer,
Edmund Kelly,	R. B. Whittemore,

    Walter Hodges.

The club has not participated in any regattas or races with other clubs, but has confined itself to the quieter exercise of steady daily pulls. Every year the circuit of Staten Island (forty miles) is made four or five times, the quickest time for the distance (five hours and twenty minutes) having been made by the four-oared barge crew in 1884. In 1883 a day was set aside in each week for the instruction of ladies in rowing in the boats of the club, and a large number of ladies are now enrolled as members.

The present officers of the club are :—

    H. R. Kelly, President.
    A. B. Boardman, Vice-President.
    W. Hodges, Treasurer.
    J. E. Bonner, Secretary.
    E. Flash, Jr., Captain.
    B. Leaward, Lieutenant.

TRUSTEES :

H. R. Kelly,	J. E. Bonner,
R. P. G. Bucklin,	A. B. Boardman,
E. Flash, Jr.,	G. A. Post,
W. Hodges,	A. J. McDonald,

    B. Leaward.

The Clifton Boat Club.

CLIFTON, S. I.

This Club was organized in 1881, commencing with a membership of eight, which has steadily increased.

The Club House is charmingly situated at Clifton, S. I., and is a delightful place to visit during the boating season. The house is 66 feet deep by 35 feet wide, with a 12 feet piazza on two sides, facing the Narrows.

This Club was started as a social organization, and until last year when a barge crew was sent to compete in the Kill Von Kull Regatta, has not taken part in rowing regattas open to other Clubs.

The crew sent last year had practically little or no training, and they were entered more because the Club had joined the Association than for any other reason, but although handicapped by a heavy barge, they pushed the Arthur-Kulls from start to finish, and made so plucky a fight against big odds that the Club was convinced the material was *there*, and all that was needed was a boat worthy of their *mettle*. Hereafter good work may be expected from the Cliftons, and they will undoubtedly prove dangerous rivals for "Kill Von Kull" honors at the annual Regattas.

Last September the Cliftons held a Fair for their benefit which cleared the handsome sum of $1,329.50, and this, together with good management, has placed the Club in excellent financial condition. The present membership is 75, and the value of the house and other property about $6,000. The Club has purchased some new boats, and now owns

   1 Six-oared Barge,
   1 Four-oared Gig,
   1 Paired-oared Gig,
   12 Singles,
   and 2 4-oared Barges.

The following comprise the officers for the year 1885 :—

  I. K. Martin, President.
  W. Hodges, Vice-President.
  Gregory McKean, Secretary.
  S. Howard Martin, Treasurer.
  George A. Post, Captain.
  Arthur D. F. Wright, Lieutenant.

BOARD OF TRUSTEES :

N. Marsh,	B. B. Hopkins,
W. B. McKean,	C. M. Dodge,
C. Barton.	

The Bayonne Canoe Club.

BAYONNE.

The Bayonne Canoe Club was organized on May 2, 1882, by Messrs. E. R. Smith, R. V. Vienot, F. B. Collins, A. F. Fleming, and A. F. Burke, and since that time it has grown steadily until this year it became necessary to increase the size of the Club House in order to accommodate the members and the fleet of canoes.

The Club House is pleasantly situated between the Newark Bay Boat Club House and the old Randall property, and the "boys" are very proud of it, as indeed, they ought to be.

The Club fleet at present consists of eleven handsome canoes, which present a very pretty sight when the Club is on a cruise. with colors flying and the boys rigged to take the weather as they find it.

New members are being initiated at every meeting, and before next season begins it is probably that the "fleet" will be increased.

The Regattas of the Canoe Club have always been very interesting, attracting numerous spectators who have been well paid for the trouble. The note of preparation had already been sounded early in the spring. The Regatta took place on July 4, and the Club had a gala time on that occasion. If the members continue to work harmoniously they will probably be able to add a second story to their Club House next year. This will be a much needed improvement, as it will give them plenty of room for Club meetings and the entertainment of their friends. We understand that the "Ariels" have been invited to give them a benefit performance at an early date in aid of the building fund, and we hope this will be largely attended, as our young neighbors are deserving of success.

The following are the officers for 1885:—

> Geo. W. Heard, Commodore.
> Louis F. Burke, Vice-Commodore,
> Fred. B. Collins, Sec'y and Treas.

HINTS ON CANOEING.

No sport has more devoted adherents. Healthy, agreeable, exciting at times, full of novelty and variety, canoeing offers a large range of attractions to its votaries, and it is seldom that one who has once felt its spell recovers from its general influence. There are many models and varieties of canoes, but they may all be reduced to two classes: the paddling canoe, of which the Rob Roy is the type, and the sailing canoe, of which the Shadow is perhaps the most generally used in this country. Both carry sails and both are paddled, but the paddling canoe usually—though not always—carries less sail than the sailing canoe, and is more easily paddled, since she is smaller and lighter. Fourteen feet is the length of the great majority of canoes, though Rob Roys are twelve feet, and sailing canoes of sixteen are not uncommon. A fourteen-foot Rob-Roy ought not to weigh over fifty-five pounds, and a fourteen-foot shadow which weighs over seventy-five pounds is unnecessarily heavy. Canoes are usually built of wood, although cheap canoes can be built of canvas, and certain advantages are claimed for those built of paper. The true object for which the canoe is built is cruising. Hence she is made so light that she can be carried around obstacles by the canoeists; so strong that she will bear the rough work of running shallow rapids; so seaworthy that she can brave the rough waters of large lakes; so commodious that her owner can sleep on board of her and carry plenty of stores, and so beautiful that every stranger will admire her and be proud to aid the lofty purpose of the canoeist. No canoe which is not fitted for cruising is a true canoe. She may be a good sailboat, or a good paddling machine, but she is not a good canoe.

The canoeist must, of course, learn how to paddle and how to sail; but paddling and sailing, to quote the words of an expert, "are only branches of canoeing. He must learn to be a boatbuilder, for he may at any time have to repair his own canoe himself. He must learn to be a sailmaker, for he will always be trying to make improvements in the rig of his canoe. He must learn to cook—in which science are included the problems of building a fire with wet wood and of finding provisions in a wilderness. He must learn geography with a minuteness with which only the man can learn who personally explores streams on which no boat, except a canoe, has ever floated. He must learn the art of running rapids and detecting at a glance where the channel through them lies—an art which, more than any other art or any known science, develops decision of character. He must learn that wet and cold and heat and damp are of no consequence, and can even be made sources of delight. And, above all, he must learn to bear with the infirmities of the canoeist who cruises in company with him, and never to shirk his rightful turn of duty in connection with scouring the frying-pan."

ATHLETIC NOTES AND FACTS.
1885.

The Season for Field Athletics for 1885 really closed with the decision of the events on Election Day, and altogether the year has been one of general satisfaction to the Athletes and Clubs in general.
The visit of L. E. Myers to England, where he again demonstrated his superiority over the runners of that country, had the effect of increasing the respect held there for our Champions, and the retirement of the American phenomenon is another happening that will make the season memorable. Apart from Myers's participation in the events of the year, they were made interesting by the reorganization of the "Williamsburgh Athletic Club" under the name of the ' Brooklyn Athletic Association;" the Myers Testimonial Athletic Benefit under the management of Mr. G. H. Badeau, President of the Williamsburgh A. C.; Mr. G. W. Carr, President of the Manhattan A. C.; Mr. J. W. Edwards, President of the Staten Island A. C., and Mr. William Wood, Treasurer of the New York A. C., and the "split" in the American Athletic Club, and the organization of the seceders under the name of the Olympic Athletic Club. Like all young Clubs, the Olympic has made steady progress, has produced many new men of note, and has secured a fair share of prizes offered in the open competitions. At present the Olympic is an Athletic Club, pure and simple, with none of the social element that slowly but surely causes a club to become athletic only in game.
The social element in Clubs is like "dry rot," and eats into the vitals of Athletic Clubs, and soon causes them to fail in the purpose for which they were organized. It was so with the old Harlem Athletic Club, which produced the fastest runners and walkers from 1876 to 1880. It was so with the Scottish-American, the Astoria, the Short Hills, the Orion, Plainfield and other Clubs which are known by name only, if at all, to the Amateur Clubs of the present day. It has been noticable in the American Club for some time, is a prime factor in the New York, and is apparently entering the Manhattan. It is like an octopus that squeezes the life-blood out of the organization by burdening it with debt. Palatial club-houses are erected at great cost and money is spent in adorning them that, if used to beautify athletic grounds and improve tracks, would cause a wide-spread interest in athletic sports and further the development of the wind and muscles of American youths. About five years ago athletic sports were at their zenith, since then they have been on the decline. The youths who participate in health-giving competitions, as a rule, cannot afford the expense of membership to the so-called Athletic Clubs and they retire in favor of the wealthy young man whose sole claim to athletic distinction is his connection with a "high-toned" club.

SHREWSBURY
Tomatoketchup
A TABLE LUXURY.

THE FIRST TOMATOKETCHUP EVER PLACED ON THE MARKET, MADE ENTIRELY FROM EARLY RIPE TOMATOES.

Shrewsbury Tomatoketchup is the pure expressed Fruit of the Red Apple Tomato, a variety of Tomato originally from the high table-lands of South America, first brought to Shrewsbury, New Jersey, where by careful selection of seed and fine culture it has been brought to great perfection.

The fruit is allowed to thoroughly ripen on the vines before being picked. It is then crushed and carefully prepared so as not to injure the color or in any way tend to dissipate its natural flavor and spicy aroma.

It excites the appetite, promotes digestion, and is pronounced by connoisseurs one of the finest condiments for use with hot and cold meats, game, fish, and oyster stews, and in giving a superior flavor to gravies or any delicate preparation of meat. With lamb and veal chops it is simply delicious, and is a great addition to maccaroni or hot buttered toast.

Do not reduce its consistency with vinegar, or mix with any other preparation of ketchup. Should the bottle be accidently left uncorked, it will not mould or lose its flavor.

Guaranteed to keep in any climate.

E. C. HAZARD & CO.

FACTORY: Shrewsbury, New Jersey, near Long Branch,

STORES—192—194 CHAMBERS ST., NEW YORK.

THE
BECKETT & McDOWELL
Manufacturing Co.
ENGINEERS, IRON FOUNDERS
——AND——
MACHINISTS,

MANUFACTURERS OF

Steam Engines and Mining Machinery,

No. 120 LIBERTY ST.,

NEW YORK.

Works, Arlington, New Jersey

CALL AT

RENTON BROS.,

101 E. NINTH STREET,

And see their fine stock of

Boats, Canoes, Oars Paddles, Rowlocks, Fittings, Etc., Etc.

Quality the Best,
            Prices the Lowest.

If you cannot call, you certainly should have a copy of their new Illustrated Catalogue containing nearly two hundred cuts, the most unique thing of the kind ever gotten out.

Send ten cents in stamps and get a copy. It will prove a good investment.

RENTON BROS.,
101 E. Ninth Street,
NEW YORK.

It is to be hoped that this book will now accomplish its purpose, which is to forward in this country,

AMERICAN

AMATEUR

ATHLETICS.

BUY YOUR JERSEYS, STOCKINGS, AND GENERAL SPORTING GOODS, OF **SMITH,** 123 FULTON ST., IN HAT STORE - UP-STAIRS, LOWEST PRICES.

NOTICE.

Having presented 5,000 Copies to be circulated among the Members of the leading Athletic Clubs, notice is hereby given that additional Copies are for sale, and may be obtained of the publisher,

CHAS. R. BOURNE,

No. 100 William St.,

Or by addressing   N. Y. City.

Mr. F. W. JANSSEN,

P. O. Box 12

Price 25 cents.   N. Y. City.

www.ingramcontent.com/pod-product-compliance
Lightning Source LLC
Chambersburg PA
CBHW020138170426
43199CB00010B/796